T0351999

CANON FIRE

Edited by
Michael Morpurgo

PAIRING CONTEMPORARY
AND **CLASSIC** TEXTS

www.heinemann.co.uk

✓ Free online support
✓ Useful weblinks
✓ 24 hour online ordering

01865 888080

Heinemann

Heinemann is an imprint of Pearson Education Limited, a company incorporated in England and Wales, having its registered office at Edinburgh Gate, Harlow, Essex, CM20 2JE. Registered company number: 872828

www.heinemann.co.uk

Heinemann is a registered trademark of Pearson Education Limited

Text © Pearson Education Limited

First published 2008

21
19

British Library Cataloguing in Publication Data is available from the British Library on request.

ISBN: 978 0 435131 94 4

Typeset by Phoenix Photosetting, Chatham, Kent
Cover design by Siu Hang Wong
Printed and bound in Great Britain by Bell and Bain Ltd, Glasgow

Disclaimer: this collection contains some uninhibited and explicit language

Acknowledgements
'The Heart of Another' by Marcus Sedgwick, from *The Restless Dead* edited by Deborah Noyes, published by Candlewick 2007. Reprinted with permission of Elizabeth Roy Agency; 'The Writing on the Wall' by Celia Rees, from *Gothic!* edited by Deborah Noyes, Candlewick Press. © Celia Rees. Reprinted with permission of Rosemary Sandberg Limited; 'The Destructors' by Graham Greene, from *Twenty-One Short Stories* by Graham Greene, published by Vintage. Reprinted with permission of David Higham Associates Limited; 'Chicken' by Mary Hoffman, from *Dare You* edited by Wendy Cooling. Copyright © Mary Hoffman. Reprinted with permission of Rogers, Coleridge & White Ltd, 20 Powis Mews, London W11 1JN; 'Porkies' by Robert Swindells, from *Ten Of The Best* edited by Wendy Cooling, published by Collins. Copyright © Robert Swindells 2002. Reprinted with permission of Jennifer Luithlen Agency; 'Billy the Kid' by William Golding from *The Hot Gates* by William Golding, published by Faber and Faber Limited. Reprinted with permission of Faber and Faber; 'The Cats' from *Shades Of Darkness* by Robert Westall, published by Macmillan. © The Estate of Robert Westall 1993, 1998. Reprinted with permission of the author's estate, via Laura Cecil Literary Agency; 'The Ugly Wife' from *Myths And Legends* by Anthony Horowitz, published by Kingfisher 1991, 2007 copyright © Anthony Horowitz 1991. Reprinted with permission of The Maggie Noach Literary Agency on behalf of the author; 'The Knight's Tale' from *The Canterbury Tales retold by Geraldine McCaughrean* (OUP 1999) Copyright © Geraldine McCaughrean 1984. Reproduced with permission of Oxford University Press; 'The Tinker's Curse' by Joan Aiken. Copyright © Joan Aiken 1989. Reprinted by permission of A. M. Heath & Co. Ltd

Contents

Folk Stories

Introduction

When you open a book of short stories, what do you want
to read? A short story. An introduction merely serves to
postpone the pleasure. Oh, I know it's expected. But
if I wrote one, most of you wouldn't bother to read it.
So instead of an introduction, I've written a short story
of my own. Because that's what I do best. The truth is,
I'd rather write a short story, than write about them. So
that's what I've done. I wrote it just as my fellow writers
in this book did, because I wanted to write it, because
I needed to write it. I had to, 'because a fire was in my
head.'

Recently I went flying kites, something I hadn't done
for years and years. I'd forgotten the jubilation of it.
Perhaps, it is the closest we ever get to fly free. That
same day I heard that a child had been shot in Palestine.
He was flying his kite when it happened. That is why
I had to write his story. Here it is. There are more to
follow, all different, stories from the great authors of the
past to the new writers of today, stories from all over the
world. They are stories I've loved reading. I hope you
will too.

Michael Morpurgo

No Trumpets Needed
Michael Morpurgo

I am a cameraman. I work freelance, working on my own. It's how I like it. I was on the West Bank a few weeks ago, my first job in the bitter cauldron of contention that is the Middle East. Of course I had seen on television, like most of us, the anguish of the grieving, the burnt-out buses, the ritual humiliation at checkpoints, the tanks in the streets, the stone-throwing crowds, the olive groves and the hill-top settlements, children playing in open sewers in the refugee camps – and now, the wall. I knew the place in images, I was there to make more of them, I suppose. But I had a more personal reason for being there too. I saw it on television, watched in disbelief as the Berlin Wall came tumbling down. It was the most hopeful, most momentous event of my young life. Now another wall had been built, and I wanted to find out about the lives of the people who lived close to it – on both sides. I began my travels on the Palestinian side.

I had been there only a couple of days when I first came across a shepherd boy. He was sitting alone on a hillside under an olive tree with his sheep grazing all around him. I had seen nothing remotely picturesque in this land until that moment, nothing until now that reminded me in any way of its biblical past. The shepherd boy was making a kite, so intent upon it that he had not noticed my approach. He was whistling softly, not to make a tune, I felt, but simply to reassure his sheep. When he did look up he showed no surprise or alarm. His smile was openhearted and engaging. I could not bring myself to pass by with a mere greeting or a paltry nod of the head.

So I sat down and offered him a drink out of my rucksack. He drank gratefully, eagerly, but said nothing. I patted my camera, told him who I was, shook his hand. I tried to communicate in English, then in the very few words of Arabic I had picked up. His smile was the only reply I got. Clearly he liked me to speak, wanted me to stay, but I knew he didn't understand a word I was saying. So, after a while I lapsed into silence and watched him at work on his kite, the sheep shifting all around us under the shade of the tree, their smell pungent and heavy in the warm air.

When I began to film him he seemed unconcerned, disinterested even. We shared what food we had. He took a great fancy to some Scottish shortbread I'd brought with me from back home in Dundee, and he gave me some of his pine nuts. And we shared our silence too, both of us knowing instinctively that this was fine, as good a way as any to get to know one another.

When evening came and he stood up and began to whistle his sheep home, I knew he expected me to go with him, like one of his sheep. Later, I found myself sitting in his house, surrounded by his huge extended family, all talking amongst each other and watching me, not with hostility, but certainly with some suspicion. It was an unsettling experience. But the boy, I noticed, still said nothing. He was showing everyone the progress he had made with his kite. I could see that he was a much treasured child. We ate lamb, and the most succulent broad beans I had ever tasted, then sweet spiced cake dripping with honey. When the boy came and sat himself down beside me, I knew he was showing me off. I was his guest, and I felt suddenly honoured by that, and moved by his affection.

Then, much to my surprise one of the men spoke to me directly, and in good English. 'I am Saïd's uncle,' he began. 'You are most welcome in our home. Saïd would want to say this himself, but he does not speak. Not any more. There was a time when you could not stop him.' He would pause from time to explain to everyone what he was telling me. 'It happened two years ago,' he went on. 'Mahmoud was flying his kite on the hill. It was before they built the wall. Mahmoud was Saïd's elder brother. He loved to make kites. He loved to fly kites. Saïd was with him. He was always with him. That day, a settler's car had been ambushed down in the valley. Three of them were killed. One was a little girl. Afterwards the soldiers came, and the helicopters. There was some shooting. Maybe it was a revenge killing. Maybe it was a stray bullet. Who knows? Who cares? Mahmoud was shot dead, and Saïd saw it all. In front of his eyes he saw it. Since this day he does not speak. Since this day he does not grow. God willing he will, God willing. Maybe he is small, maybe he cannot speak, but he is the best shepherd in all Palestine. And you make the best kites too, don't you Saïd? And Saïd's kites are not ordinary kites.'

'What do you mean?' I asked.

'Maybe he will show you that himself. Maybe he will fly this kite for you tomorrow. This one is ready to fly, I think. But the wind must always be from the east, or Saïd will not fly his kites.'

I spent the night under the stars, on the roof of the house. I was tired but far too troubled to sleep. I was up at dawn and went down into the valley. I wanted to film the sun rising over the wall. Once I'd done that I climbed back up the hill so that I could get a long shot of the wall, tracking it as it sliced obscenely through the olive groves and across the hillside beyond. Dogs barked, and cocks crowed at one another from both sides of the wall.

After breakfast I went off with Saïd and his sheep, Saïd carrying his kite, now with its string attached. I doubted he'd be flying it that day because there was very little wind. But an hour or so later, sitting on the highest hill above the village, with the sheep browsing in amongst the rocks, their bells sounding softly, I felt a sudden breeze spring up. Saïd was on his feet at once, eagerly offering me his kite. I noticed then for the first time that there was writing on one side of the kite, and a drawing too, of a dove.

He was urging me to run now, racing ahead of me to show me how to do it. I felt the wind taking it, felt the kite suddenly air-borne, wind-whipped and tugging to be free. Saïd clapped his hands in wild delight as it swooped and soared above us. I had done this on Hampstead Heath with my father when I was a boy, but had forgotten the sheer exhilaration of it. The kite was alive at the end of the string, loving it as much as I was. Saïd tapped my arm and took the string from me. Very reluctantly I handed it over.

Saïd was an expert. With a tweak of his wrist the kite turned and twirled, with a flick of his fingers he dived it and danced it. My professional instinct kicked in. I needed boy and kite in the same shot, so I had to put some distance between them and me. I backed away over the hillside, pausing to film as I went, fearful of missing these fleeting moments of innocent rapture in this war-ravaged land. I closed on the fluttering kite, then zoomed in on the wall below, following it up over the hillside, and focusing on the settlement beyond, on the flag flying there, and then on some children playing football in the street below. I watched them through my lens, witnessed the celebratory hugging as one of them scored.

I turned my camera on Saïd again. There was, I noticed, a look of intense concentration on his face. That was the moment he let the kite go. It was quite deliberate. He simply gave it to the wind, holding his arms aloft as if he'd just released a trapped bird, and was giving it its freedom. It soared up high, seeming to float there for a while on the thermals, before the wind discovered it and took it away over the olive grove, over the wall and up towards the hilltop settlement.

Saïd was tugging at my arm again. He wanted to look through my lens. I saw then what he was looking at, a young girl in a headscarf gazing up at the kite as it came floating down. Now she was running over to where it had landed. She picked it up and stood looking at us for a few moments, before the footballers came racing down the hill towards her. They all stood there then, gazing across at us. But when Saïd waved, only the girl in the headscarf waved back. They didn't fly the kite. They just took it away and disappeared.

On the way home with the sheep later that day, we came across Saïd's uncle harvesting his broad beans. 'It's a poor crop, but what can you do?' he said. 'There is never enough water. They take all our best land, all our water. They leave us only the dust to farm in.' I stayed to talk while Saïd walked on up into the village with his sheep. 'So the wind was right,' Saïd's uncle went on. 'Saïd never keeps his kites you know, not one. He just makes them, waits for the east wind, and sends them off. Did you see what he draws on each one? A dove of peace. Did you see what he writes? Salaam. Shalom. And he signs every one of them: Mahmoud and Saïd.'

'How many has he sent?' I asked.

'A hundred maybe. About one a week since they killed Mahmoud. He wrote it down for his mother once, telling her why he does it. For Saïd, every kite that lands over there, is like a seed of friendship. He believes that one day they'll send the kites back, and everything will be right, friendships will grow, and peace will come and the killing will stop. Let him have his dreams. It's all he has. He'll find out soon enough what they're like over there.'

'There was a girl who found the kite,' I told him. 'She waved back. I saw her. It's a beginning.'

'It costs nothing to wave,' he replied bitterly.

I stayed one more night. So I was there to see the embryo of the next kite taking shape, Saïd kneeling on the carpet, his whole family watching intently as he constructed the frame with infinite care, ignoring all their advice, and the food and drink they constantly offered him. 'Maybe it is good,' Saïd's uncle said to me, when Saïd had gone up to bed, 'maybe it helps him to forget. Maybe if he forgets, he will find his voice again. Maybe he will grow again. God willing. God willing.'

I said my goodbyes early the next morning and left with Saïd and the sheep. Saïd held my hand all the way. There was between us, I felt, the same unspoken thought: that we were friends and did not want to part, and that when we did we would probably never see each other again. The sheep were in clambering mood, their bells jangling loud in the morning air. We sat down on the hillside where we'd flown the kite the day before. Saïd had brought the frame of his new kite with him, but he was not in the mood for working on it. Like me he was gazing out over the valley, over the wall, towards the settlement. The flag still fluttered there. A donkey brayed balefully nearby, winding itself up into a frenzy of misery. I felt it was time for me to go. I put my hand on Saïd's shoulder, let it rest there a few moments, then left him.

When I looked back a while later he was busy with his kite. I stopped to film him. It would be the perfect closing shot. I had just about got myself ready to film when Saïd sprang to his feet. The sheep were suddenly bounding away from him, scattering across the hillside.

Then I saw the kites. They were all colours of the rainbow, hundreds of them, like dancing butterflies they were, rising into the air from the hillside below the settlement. I could hear the shrieks of joy, saw the crowd of children gathered there, every one of them flying a kite. A few snagged each other and plunged to earth, but most sailed up triumphantly heavenwards. The settlers were pouring out of their houses to watch. One after the other, the kites were released, took wind and flew out over the wall towards us. And from behind me, from Saïd's village, the people came running too, as the kites landed in amongst us, and amongst the terrified sheep too. On every kite I saw the same message, in English and in Hebrew: 'Shalom and Salaam'. And on every kite too there was a drawing of an olive branch. Everywhere on both sides of the wall the children were cheering and laughing and dancing about. I could see the girl in the scarf waving at us, and leaping up and down.

Around me, some of the mothers and fathers, grandmothers and grandfathers, began to clap too, hesitantly at first. But others soon joined in, Saïd's uncle amongst them. But the cheering, I noticed, and the laughter and the dancing they left to the children. The hillsides rang with their jubilation, with their exultation. It seemed to me like a joyous symphony of hope.

As I raced over the hillside towards Saïd, I could hear him laughing and shouting out loud along with all the others. I realised then – idiot that I was – that I had quite forgotten to film this miracle. And almost simultaneously I understood that it didn't matter anyway, that it was the laughter that mattered. It was laughter that would one day resonate so loud that this wall would come tumbling down. No trumpets needed, as they had been at Jericho, only the laughter of children.

The Heart of Another
Marcus Sedgwick

When I woke. The first thing. Was. The Light.

It was there even before. Even before I had my eyes open. Then. I made the mistake. Of opening my eyes.

Light filled my head and I was blinded.

I didn't know where I was. Of course. I knew nothing.

It was all so hard. Even to think. Never mind to remember. I shut my eyes. Quickly.

Slowly.

Ever so slowly, things began to change. I began to think, and I began to remember.

I realised where I was. The hospital. I could smell it now, and though my eyes were shut, I could see the hospital. My white room, All around me would be wards and the nurses. Doctors.

The next thing was the pain.

Everything was a blur. My head was throbbing. My arms and legs were jelly, but somewhere there was a vast pain.

Gingerly, I moved one of my jelly arms underneath the bedclothes. I lifted a hand up across my chest, catching one breast, pulling on something.

A pain speared through my chest and the white light went black.

I don't know how long it was before I woke again.

It was dark now, and for a moment I thought I'd gone blind somehow. That was the first time I began to panic. Not because I thought I'd gone blind, but because I knew I was thinking irrationally. But maybe it was a good sign. Maybe it was the first time I'd been well enough to think, even if those thoughts were irrational.

It might have been the evening of the same day I first woke. It might have been a week later. I had no way of telling.

I could still feel the pain between my breasts, and this time, I moved carefully, lifting my jelly hand high, and then inching it back toward my chest.

Yes, there it was. A thick dressing running down my breastbone. I rested a finger on it as lightly as I could. The pain howled into me again and I lay back on the pillow, cowering, waiting for the sharpness to return to a dull ache.

A single word floated into my head, and I knew it was a word that had been spoken over my unconscious body, many times, like a prayer. An invocation.

The word was a strange one. *Cyclosporine.*

I tried it on my tongue, whispering into the dark.

'Cyclo. Sporine.'

I couldn't remember what it meant, but I knew it was of enormous importance to me. Now.

I lay in the dark. Waiting for someone to come.

No one came.

Before I knew I was asleep, I found myself waking again.

The pain was less. And now real thoughts ran through me. Real thoughts. The ones that make us human. Desires and fears.

My first fear was for my work. Ever since they found as a baby that I had a bad heart, I suppose I'd been waiting for the operation to happen. And it had to happen seventeen years later, just as I was trying to get my thesis together. The last year had been a mess, as my heart that had never been made properly started to give out.

There'd been a few scares. I nearly didn't make it a couple of times. But I kept working when I could. It was only thanks to John, my tutor, that I'd gotten anywhere at all. But my parents had been pressing for the operation – I knew that. I knew I couldn't fight it off forever, though I didn't want to admit it. The Speculations of Edgar Allan Poe would have to wait,

I told my parents I didn't want to interrupt my thesis, but the real reason was simpler than that, I was scared. Finally I couldn't hold out anymore, but things weren't that simple. I'd only been thinking about me, what I wanted and what I didn't want. But I'd forgotten that for the operation to happen at all, we needed something else.

A compatible thing.

Of the right tissue type.

And it seemed that in the whole Bay Area, no one was dying with the kind of heart I needed. So I lay in the hospital, getting closer and closer to death.

Until finally someone died, and saved me.

At some point they'd removed the dressing from my chest, and now I could run my fingers down the scar. Miserably I wondered if it would ever heal well enough so it didn't show. It would be something to explain to my boyfriend, if I ever had one. And as I pondered a sex life I might never have, a different kind of desire crept into me.

Suddenly, from nowhere, came an overwhelming need for a long, cool glass of beer.

Which was very strange because I have always hated beer.

⚫ ⚫ ⚫ ⚫

Those first days seem so far away now. It was a strange time. A long blur of light and dark, of pain and numbness. Things are much clearer now. I can think again. In fact, I was thinking clearly well before I was allowed out. That was the worst time. So frustrating, when all I wanted to do was get back to my work.

My parents came to see me during that time. I'd asked them to bring my books. At the very least, I begged for Poe's *Tales of Mystery and Imagination*. Yes, I'd read them all a dozen times, but I still had to focus myself on them. On him. They brought me no books. They brought me a magazine.

Mother looked worried, Dad looked at Mother, almost as if I weren't there.

'Are you taking your pills?' Mother said.

'What do you think?' I snapped, then regretted it. She began to wring her hands. I knew she felt my condition was her fault. And maybe it was.

'They bring it in three times a day,' I said, trying to be nicer. 'Twenty-five milligrams of cyclosporine. There's no way I'll be allowed to forget.'

'You need it, darling.'

I smiled at them and told them I was fine.

They left. I threw the magazine across the room, then collapsed on my pillows, wincing.

A couple of days later I had another visitor. John Reynolds, my tutor. He was even taller than I remembered him, but otherwise he was your average professor of English. Middle-aged. Messy hair, poor dress sense. Good-looking, though, I admit.

'You look well,' he said, smiling down at me. I could tell he was lying, but it was good of him to say it. I waved a hand limply.

'Yeah, you know....'

He said nothing. Just stared at me.

'So where were you, John? I've been here for days, and–'

He held up his hand.

'I'm sorry,' he said. 'I'm sorry. I was at the Funkdorf Convention in Geneva. I told you all April was pretty much wiped out. Got back two days ago. There was a lot to do...'

I said nothing, still angry at him for abandoning me.

'I have something for you,' he said, and pulled a book from his bag.

'How did you know?'

I forgot to be angry anymore; it was the *Tales of Mystery and Imagination*.

'Let's just say I guessed. Don't think I want you working hard. You need to take it easy. But you're the best student I've ever had, and that thesis won't wait forever. A little light reading until you're ready to get back to Edgar properly.'

I smiled and put the book down on the bed beside me. It had become too heavy to hold.

'Do you know where you're going to take it yet?'

I laughed.

'I thought you didn't want me working hard.'

He shrugged. 'Just a question.'

'Well, I think I'm going to try to pull one of the tales apart. Break it down and build it up again. I'm going to analyse sentence structure, paragraph length, and vocab. But more important than that, I'm going to propose that you can find the essence of Poe in any of his stories. His style, his ideas, his structures. That everything that is him is to be found in all his work. Like a fingerprint.'

'Sounds good,' John said. 'Sounds very good. But which tale are you going to use?'

'"The Tell-Tale Heart,"' I said, and even as I said it, I knew it had to be that one. That was a strange thing, because up to that point I had had no idea.

John shrugged.

'Okay,' he said. He turned to the window – a little awkwardly, I thought.

'Soon be summer,' he said.

'Perfect for a fishing trip across the bay,' I said.

He turned from the window.

'What?'

'Nothing,' I said.

'I didn't know you liked fishing.'

'I don't,' I said. 'I just thought...'

I trailed off. John said nothing.

He made to leave.

'You're taking your cyclosporine?'

I laughed.

'Yes,' I said.

'You know you need it, so your body ... accepts your new heart.'

'Yes,' I said, but still smiling patiently. 'I get that lecture three times a day from the nurses.'

He went.

I looked down at the book he'd brought me. I put a hand on it, but I was too tired to pick it up.

I closed my eyes, and then it hit me.

Yes. I had to take my cyclosporine because the heart in my chest wasn't mine, and my body might reject it otherwise.

It might reject it because it came from someone else.

I had someone else's heart inside me, and the heart of another is a dark forest.

'The Tell-Tale Heart.' Once I'd said it to John, it had to be that story. It had everything I needed for my thesis, and I knew it would yield to the rigorous analysis I had planned for it. But why that story? There were others just as useful for my purposes.

The story features a wild narrator, obsessive, and yet his narration displays an apparent logic. The narrator kills the old man in whose house he lodges and carries off the deed with chilling efficiency. He seems to have gotten away with the crime, and even when the police come to search the house, having heard reports of a shriek, he convinces them that all is well. But the narrator is convinced that he can still hear the old man's heart beating. The beating gets louder and louder, and the killer can't understand why the police can't hear it. Finally his mind snaps and he confesses – pointing toward the floorboards where the old man's body lies.

What he never understands is why the police seem to be ignoring the loud and frantic beating of the heart.

The narrator is, of course, mad.

And the thing about madmen is that they don't know they're mad.

The dreams started when I got home. My initial delight at being freed from the hospital died that very first night. It had been awful, stuck in that white, white room, for day after day after day. I read the *Tales of Mystery and Imagination* from cover to cover so many times I lost count. When I got a little stronger, I began to make notes for my thesis, but nothing could prevent the awful spaces of boredom that filled my days.

My parents drove me home and walked slowly beside me as I made my way up the stairs. Three flights and I was exhausted, but I put on a brave face so they wouldn't worry, and after a while, I managed to get them to leave.

As soon as they'd gone, I collapsed on the sofa and slept all afternoon. When I woke, it was dusk. I got up for a bit and wandered around my apartment as if it belonged to someone else. It had been so long, everything was unfamiliar and so different from the whiteness of the room. At first it was hard to take it all in. The colours, the browns – chairs, my desk, the floorboards. The spines of books on the shelves. The shiny things in the kitchen, the soft things in the bedroom.

After an hour of this aimlessness, I felt overwhelmed by tiredness again and went to bed. I undressed and looked at myself naked in the bedroom mirror. The scar was much better, but I knew then that it would always be there. I pulled on a nightshirt and went to bed. And that's when the dreams started.

The first thing is the pain. Pain searing across my chest. Then there is the light, not bright and all-encompassing, but a single beam blazing in a darkened space. Then there's the crack as my breastbone is split in two. By now I should have passed out from the pain, but I don't. I see a knife slide into me, slitting the pericardium. My heart is exposed. Someone reaches their hands toward it.

That's when I wake, screaming.

It's what I'd been thinking deep down but had refused to acknowledge. My heart is not my own. Yes, it's true that they left in a small piece of my own weak organ, but the thing that does the work now, that pumps my blood, is someone else's. It's something I haven't wanted to think about, but I can't push it away anymore.

I wonder whose it was.

Man or woman? How old were they? And, the one question that for some reason bothers me the most – how did they die?

And supposing, just supposing, this dead person isn't happy that I've got their heart. Suppose they want it back?

I got a little stronger each day, but having been confined to that white room for so long, I now found myself confined to my own apartment. I had to arrange to have groceries delivered, because I didn't even have the strength to get to the corner shop and back. So I stayed at my desk, reading 'The Tell-Tale Heart' again and again.

And just as I had told John, I pulled it apart. I think, in fact, I dissected it, like a surgeon with a scalpel. I came to know every word. I produced ratios of word length to sentence length, sentence length to paragraph length, I distilled Edgar Allan Poe to a sequence of numbers. But my frustration grew, because despite all my analysis, I felt no closer to being able to write a single word of my thesis.

John would stop by from time to time, bring me books I needed from the library, return those I had finished with.

One day, he looked at me strangely.

'What's wrong?' he said, so simply that I couldn't keep it in any longer. I told him about the dreams. It all flooded out and I felt like a fool, but he listened seriously.

'It's not that hard to understand,' he said when I had finished. 'You had a major surgical operation – just about as big as they come in fact. What you're having is an anxiety dream about the operation.'

Even as he said it, I knew that wasn't quite right, but I felt better for having unburdened myself, and I decided to let it drop.

'What I need,' I said, 'is a drink. Want a beer?'

He stood up, smiling.

'Thanks,' he said. 'But I've got too much work to mark from students less able than you.'

I blushed and showed him out.

When he'd gone, I thought about what he'd said.

There was something wrong with it; I just couldn't place it.

Not yet.

But that night, when I had the dream yet again and woke, I woke without screaming, because I had realised that the dream wasn't about me at all. It was about him – the man who'd died and whose heart I was now in possession of.

Even as I woke, I'd woken somehow knowing that it was a man's heart.

* * * *

Days went by, and I got stronger. I still had the dreams, but they no longer scared me. Every night, without fail, I found myself reliving the same sequence. At first I had found it terrifying, then only disturbing, then just unpleasant. The fact was the operation I experienced nightly was not my own, but the man's; his heart was being removed to give to me. The two processes were almost the mirror of each other; it was just that mine was a little less brutal than his. A little.

And as the nights passed, my horror became transformed into something else: sympathy.

One day, as I'd spent all morning at my desk and failed to do anything productive at all, something suddenly happened to me. I stared at the work in front of me, and it was dull and boring. I pushed it away, slid my chair from the desk, and walked to the window. I pulled the curtains wide, and light flooded into the room. It was a burning summer's day, and I threw the windows open so sharply they slammed against the walls outside.

There was the whole city in front of me, and beyond, I could see the sun glinting on the sea. I imagined what it would be like to take a boat out across the bay and feel the water and the sun and the wind. What it would be like to pull a bright wet fish into the bottom of the boat and see it flap.

I left the apartment for the first time.

That day was incredible to me.

All my life, I'd laboured with a failing heart. I'd never walked farther than a mile before, and yet, that day, I walked clear across the city and down to the bay. I swam in a small cove I discovered, and I never even stopped to think that I'd never learned to swim.

It got dark before I returned, and still I could have kept on walking. I felt stronger than I'd ever felt, and for the first time I appreciated what an amazing gift I'd been given. I had been given a life that had been closed to me before.

I was a new person. Thanks to a dead man.

My euphoria was short-lived, however, because that night was when the darkness rolled in. I had a different dream, and it was terrible. This wasn't a dream about the autopsy anymore; this was a dream about how he died. He wasn't an old man. He was a young man. I felt it all as if I were there, as if I were him. He was a young man, and he didn't die easily or from an accident.

He was killed.

He was murdered.

I woke, and I cried until dawn.

Days passed. I looked at my work less and less, and spent more and more time outside. Walking, running. I got myself a gym membership, and I became stronger. As I ran, I would think about him. My life giver. The man whose heart I was using to full capacity. I felt such sorrow for him, yet how could I regret what had happened? For without it, I would be dead.

One day, out running, I passed the city library, and something clicked in my head. Something inside the building screamed at me, and I felt a tug that I hadn't felt in weeks – the desire to learn, the desire to study, the desire to know.

Inside, I knew right away where the pull was coming from. I sailed up to the third floor – the floor where few people go – the periodical collections.

Four months ago, more or less. April I5.

I began to read, slowly at first, but then more and more frantically. I found something in the *Gazette*. Then another story in the *Bay Times*. Then with a shock I found another one a few days before. I went further back and found one weeks before that.

My heart grew cold.

I grabbed all the papers I wanted to look at again and walked downstairs and straight out of the library, ignoring the old lady at the desk shouting at me.

I went home and spread everything out on the floor.

I discarded all the pages of the papers I didn't need, and yet there were still enough to fill the living-room floor. A carpet of death.

The intercom buzzed, and I nearly hit the ceiling.

'Yes?' I said impatiently.

'It's John.'

'Thank God,' I said. 'If it had been Mother...'

I buzzed the door.

A minute later he was in my apartment.

'What are you doing?' he asked, seeing the paper on the floor.

I shrugged.

'Are you all right?' he asked.

'Yes, fine. Why?'

He hesitated.

'I haven't seen you at college, and...'

'You know I've been stuck here,' I began, but even as I said it, I knew it was a stupid thing to say.

'You've been seen everywhere around the city. Running. Everywhere, but at college.'

'You're hurt?' I said. He had such a stupid look on his face, as if he cared about me.

'We haven't seen a word of your thesis. Time is running out.'

'I'm working on it.' I said defensively.

'Is this part of it?' John said, waving a hand at the cuttings from the papers.

'No, but...'

'I stuck my neck out for you, because I believe you are the best student I've ever had. With all your health problems over the years, it wasn't easy. I just need to see some results. Some work.'

I said nothing. What could I say? I was guilty. I'd been well enough to run five miles every morning, but I hadn't opened a book in weeks.

'What is all this, anyway?' John asked.

I saw a chance to excuse myself.

'Don't start,' I said. 'It's not been easy. The operation has changed me. I dream...'

'They haven't stopped?'

'No. They got worse. Listen, John, the thing is. About my heart. I've dreamed about my heart. I know how I got it. It was murder, John. *Murder!* It's been filling my brain – I couldn't concentrate on Poe anymore. I went to the library and found all these.'

'What are they?'

I could see him looking at me strangely.

'Murders. Reports of murders in the area. Around the time of my operation. Young people, in every case. There's even a story about the high number of murders that had been happening, more than normal. The police were baffled, it says.'

'What of it?'

'One of them is mine. One of them is my heart. I think I know which one. It all makes sense...'

John shifted and moved around the floor, looking at the paper cuttings. He shook his head.

'I think maybe you've been working too hard,' he said.

'You've just told me I haven't been working at all!' I shouted suddenly.

'Listen, I just think you've been through a lot. This is all very fascinating stuff, but you shouldn't think about it like this.'

'Why not?' I snapped. 'Why shouldn't I? Someone died for me! Someone was murdered! Without that fact, I'd be dead. I just want to know who it was.'

John raised his hand, trying to calm me down.

'Don't be like this,' he said. 'Please. You shouldn't upset yourself. Like I said before, a heart transplant is a major operation and some ... mental trauma afterward is only natural.'

'You don't believe me?'

'It's not a question of whether I believe you. I just think you should leave the man who died out of this. It won't do any good....'

'What did you say?'

John said nothing, and I knew he was replaying what he had said.

'How did you know it was a man?' I asked. 'I didn't tell you that.'

'What—?' he said quickly. 'It was … just a guess. An assumption.'

But I knew he was lying. In that moment, I knew.

I bent over and picked up one of the pages, and I read, all the while keeping an eye on John's face.

' "Police today are investigating the apparently motiveless murder of a young man from the city area. The man's wallet was still on his person, including money, plastic, and even his donor card. The twenty-four-year-old was found in the early hours of yesterday morning, killed by a single shot to the head. He was a dockworker, from the fishing houses, and a fitness fanatic, according to his friends, one of whom said, 'I can't believe he won't be there for a beer after work, like usual.' Police say they have no leads at present." '

Then I knew for sure.

I looked at John.

You're my best student – that's what he'd said.

'How many did you have to kill, John? I was at the top of the waiting list for a heart. How many did you have to kill before they found one with the right tissue type?'

'Don't be absurd...'

'Did you ask them if they had a donor card before you killed them?'

'The Tell-Tale Heart.' Remember that story – the one with the mad narrator? My heart had told a tale. My heart had found its murderer. He tried to deny it. He grabbed the clipping from my hand as we argued. He looked at the date. He tried to tell me that he was at the convention in Geneva when the dockworker had been murdered. But I didn't believe him. He must have set it all up somehow. Oh, yes, I knew better than to fall for that.

I.

Knew.

He told me I was mad, that I'd lost my mind.

But I know I'm not mad.

Not.

Me.

But there's something I don't know.

I don't really know which of us did it.

I know it was me who caught John by the arm as he tried to leave the apartment. And it was me who held him on the floor while my hands closed around his neck and stayed there until he stopped shuddering.

But I don't know whether it was me or my heart that really killed him.

I guess the police will decide.

John was a tall man. And strong.

A small woman. Like me.

Could never. Have killed someone.

Like him.

Could she?

The Tell-Tale Heart
Edgar Allan Poe

True! – nervous – very, very dreadfully nervous I had been and am; but why *will* you say that I am mad? The disease had sharpened my senses – not destroyed – not dulled them. Above all was the sense of hearing acute. I heard all things in the heaven and in the earth. I heard many things in hell. How, then, am I mad? Hearken! and observe how healthily – how calmly I can tell you the whole story.

It is impossible to say how first the idea entered my brain; but once conceived, it haunted me day and night. Object there was none. Passion there was none. I loved the old man. He had never wronged me. He had never given me insult. For his gold I had no desire. I think it was his eye! yes, it was this! One of his eyes resembled that of a vulture – a pale blue eye, with a film over it. Whenever it fell upon me, my blood ran cold; and so by degrees – very gradually – I made up my mind to take the life of the old man, and thus rid myself of the eye for ever.

Now this is the point. You fancy me mad. Madmen know nothing. But you should have seen *me*. You should have seen how wisely I proceeded – with what caution – with what foresight – with what dissimulation I went to work! I was never kinder to the old man than during the whole week before I killed him. And every night, about midnight, I turned the latch of his door and opened it – oh so gently! And then, when I had made an opening sufficient for my head, I put in a dark lantern, all closed, closed, so that no light shone out, and then I thrust in my head. Oh, you would have laughed to see how cunningly I thrust it in! I moved it slowly – very, very slowly, so that I might not disturb the old man's sleep. It took me an hour to place my whole head within the opening so far that I could see him as he lay upon his bed. Ha! – would a madman have been so wise as this? And then, when my head was well in the room, I undid the lantern, cautiously – oh, so cautiously – cautiously (for the hinges creaked) I undid it just so much that a single thin ray fell upon the vulture eye. And this I did for seven long nights – every night just at midnight – but I found the eye always closed, and so it was impossible to do the work; for it was not the old man who vexed me, but his Evil Eye. And every morning, when the day broke, I went boldly into the chamber, and spoke courageously to him, calling him by name in a hearty tone, and inquiring how he had passed the night. So you see he would have been a very profound old man, indeed, to suspect that every night, just at twelve, I looked in upon him while he slept.

Upon the eighth night I was more than usually cautious in opening the door. A watch's minute hand moves more quickly than did mine. Never before that night had I felt the extent of my own powers – of my **sagacity**. I could scarcely contain my feelings of triumph. To think that there I was, opening the door, little by little, and he not even to dream of my secret deeds or thoughts. I fairly chuckled at the idea; and perhaps he heard me – for he moved on the bed suddenly, as if startled. Now you may think that I drew back – but no. His room was as black as pitch with the thick darkness (for the shutters were close fastened, through fear of robbers), and so I knew that he could not see the opening of the door, and I kept pushing it on steadily, steadily.

I had my head in, and was about to open the lantern, when my thumb slipped upon the tin fastening, and the old man sprang up in the bed, crying out, 'Who's there?'

---

sagacity wisdom

I kept quite still and said nothing. For a whole hour I did not move a muscle, and in the meantime I did not hear him lie down. He was still sitting up in the bed, listening – just as I have done, night after night, hearkening to the **deathwatches** in the wall.

Presently I heard a slight groan, and I knew it was the groan of mortal terror. It was not a groan of pain or of grief – oh, no! – it was the low stifled sound that arises from the bottom of the soul when overcharged with awe. I knew the sound well. Many a night, just at midnight, when all the world slept, it has welled up from my own bosom, deepening, with its dreadful echo, the terrors that distracted me. I say I knew it well. I knew what the old man felt, and pitied him, although I chuckled at heart, I knew that he had been lying awake ever since the first slight noise, when he had turned in the bed. His fears had been ever since growing upon him. He had been trying to fancy them causeless, but could not. He had been saying to himself, 'It is nothing but the wind in the chimney – it is only a mouse crossing the floor,' or, 'It is merely a cricket which has made a single chirp.' Yes, he had been trying to comfort himself with these suppositions; but he had found all in vain. *All in vain*, because Death, in approaching him, had stalked with his black shadow before him, and enveloped the victim. And it was the mournful influence of the unperceived shadow that caused him to feel – although he neither saw nor heard – to *feel* the presence of my head within the room.

When I had waited a long time, very patiently, without hearing him lie down, I resolved to open a little – a very, very little crevice in the lantern. So I opened it – you cannot imagine how stealthily, stealthily – until, at length, a single dim ray, like

---

deathwatches beetles that burrow into wood and make a tapping sound

the thread of the spider, shot from out the crevice and fell upon the vulture eye.

It was open – wide, wide open – and I grew furious as I gazed upon it. I saw it with perfect distinctness – all a dull blue, with a hideous veil over it that chilled the very marrow in my bones; but I could see nothing else of the old man's face or person, for I had directed the ray, as if by instinct, precisely upon the damned spot.

And have I not told you that what you mistake for madness is but over acuteness of the senses? – now, I say, there came to my ears a low, dull, quick sound, such as a watch makes when enveloped in cotton. I knew *that* sound well, too. It was the beating of the old man's heart. It increased my fury, as the beating of a drum stimulates the soldier into courage.

But even yet I refrained and kept still. I scarcely breathed. I held the lantern motionless. I tried how steadily I could maintain the ray upon the eye. Meantime the hellish tattoo of the heart increased. It grew quicker and quicker, and louder and louder every instant. The old man's terror must have been extreme! It grew louder, I say, louder every moment! – do you mark me well? I have told you that I am nervous: so I am. And now, at the dead hour of the night, amid the dreadful silence of that old house, so strange a noise as this excited me to uncontrollable terror. Yet, for some minutes longer, I refrained and stood still. But the beating grew louder, louder! I thought the heart must burst. And now a new anxiety seized me – the sound would be heard by a neighbour! The old man's hour had come! With a loud yell I threw open the lantern and leaped into the room. He shrieked once – once only. In an instant I dragged him to the floor, and pulled the heavy bed over him. I then smiled gaily, to find the deed so far done. But, for many minutes, the heart beat on with a muffled sound. This, however, did not vex me;

it would not be heard through the wall. At length it ceased. The old man was dead. I removed the bed and examined the corpse. Yes, he was stone, stone dead. I placed my hand upon the heart and held it there many minutes. There was no pulsation. He was stone dead. His eye would trouble me no more.

If still you think me mad, you will think so no longer when I describe the wise precautions I took for the concealment of the body. The night waned, and I worked hastily, but in silence. First of all I dismembered the corpse. I cut off the head and the arms and the legs.

I then took up three planks from the flooring of the chamber, and deposited all between the **scantlings**. I then replaced the boards so cleverly, so cunningly, that no human eye – not even *his* – could have detected anything wrong. There was nothing to wash out – no stain of any kind – no blood-spot whatever. I had been too wary for that. A tub had caught all – ha! ha!

When I had made an end of these labours, it was four o'clock – still dark as midnight. As the bell sounded the hour, there came a knocking at the street door. I went down to open it with a light heart – for what had I *now* to fear? There entered three men, who introduced themselves, with perfect suavity, as officers of the police. A shriek had been heard by a neighbour during the night; suspicion of foul play had been aroused; information had been lodged at the police office, and they (the officers) had been deputed to search the premises.

I smiled – for *what* had I to fear? I bade the gentlemen welcome. The shriek, I said, was my own in a dream. The old man, I mentioned, was absent in the country. I took my visitors all over the house. I bade them search – search *well*. I led them, at length, to *his* chamber. I showed them his treasures, secure, undisturbed.

---

scantlings beams that support floorboards

In the enthusiasm of my confidence, I brought chairs into the room, and desired them *here* to rest from their fatigues, while I myself, in the wild audacity of my perfect triumph, placed my own seat upon the very spot beneath which reposed the corpse of the victim.

The officers were satisfied. My *manner* had convinced them. I was singularly at ease. They sat, and while I answered cheerily, they chatted of familiar things. But, ere long, I felt myself getting pale and wished them gone. My head ached, and I fancied a ringing in my ears; but still they sat and still chatted. The ringing became more distinct – it continued and became more distinct. I talked more freely to get rid of the feeling; but it continued and gained definitiveness – until, at length, I found that the noise was *not* within my ears.

No doubt I now grew *very* pale; but I talked more fluently, and with a heightened voice. Yet the sound increased – and what could I do? It was *a low, dull, quick sound – much such a sound as a watch makes when enveloped in cotton*. I gasped for breath – and yet the officers heard it not. I talked more quickly – more vehemently, but the noise steadily increased. I arose and argued about trifles, in a high key and with violent gesticulations; but the noise steadily increased. Why *would* they not be gone? I paced the floor to and fro with heavy strides, as if excited to fury by the observations of the men – but the noise steadily increased. O God! what *could* I do? I foamed – I raved – I swore! I swung the chair upon which I had been sitting, and grated it upon the boards, but the noise arose over all and continually increased. It grew louder – louder – *louder!* And still the men chatted pleasantly, and smiled. Was it possible they heard not? Almighty God! – no, no! They heard! – they suspected! – they *knew!* – they were making a mockery of my horror! – this I thought, and this I think. But anything was better than this agony! Anything was more tolerable than this derision! I could bear those hypocritical smiles no longer! I felt that I must scream or die! – and now – again! – hark! louder! louder! louder! *louder!*

'Villains!' I shrieked, 'dissemble no more! I admit the deed! – tear up the planks! – here, here! – it is the beating of his hideous heart!'

The Writing on the Wall
Celia Rees

Mark Banks had a tendency to act on impulse; otherwise he never would have bought the place. The house stood back from the road, in the hollow of a hill. He glimpsed it through a haze of new green leaves, picked out by a random shaft of sunlight on a bright spring day. He noted the FOR SALE sign and pulled in to take a closer look. It was built from dull red brick, not particularly picturesque, but gable ends and steeply pitched roofs, banks of tall chimneys, and a fancy turret gave it a certain grandeur. A Victorian gentleman's residence, He liked the idea of that. The FOR SALE sign had been up for so long that the post was rotting, but he didn't question why that might be. He merely noted the estate agent's number and decided to give them a call. He had to smile when they told him the price. He put in an offer right over the phone. He knew a bargain when he saw one.

There was something hidden about the house, tucked away in a nook of the landscape, folded in on itself as if guarding a secret, the twin roofs of the gables rising like great arching brows frowning a warning, but Mark was not a man given to fancy. His son, Sam, was far more sensitive. He felt a definite prickle of doubt the first time his dad showed him the photographs, but he didn't share his misgivings with anyone. Who'd listen to a twelve-year-old?

There was a lot of work to be done, Mark told his family, but it was going to be fun. The estate agent had recommended a good local firm, and they were already transforming the place. The fabric was sound, the survey said, and that was enough for Mark. There are other sorts of rottenness: kinds that can't be detected by gauges measuring dampness or gadgets that find dry rot or woodworm infestation, but Mark Banks didn't stop to think about that.

He was due some time off and had decided to oversee the work himself. He liked getting his hands dirty and had definite ideas about how the place should be. There were interesting features, like a pretty little summerhouse in the garden, and there had been some fascinating finds already. Just yesterday, one of the men had found a little glass bottle, half filled with some dark, viscous liquid, hidden above the doorway. None of them seemed to know what it was, or why it was there. Mark planned to take it to the local museum as soon as he could find the time.

He'd fixed up a trailer in the garden, and now that school vacation had started, the kids would be joining him. They were both curious to see the house. Kate was fifteen and had already picked out her room from the photographs. She wanted the turret because it looked like a tower in a fairy-tale castle, and she'd wanted to sleep in one of those ever since she was a child. Not that she'd be moving in for a while. She'd be staying with him in the trailer. It was big enough for all of them, but Sam said he wanted to sleep outside so he could try out his new tent.

Sam liked the idea of camping, but on the first night he found it hard to sleep. He wasn't used to the quiet, and each time he closed his eyes, there would be some unfamiliar noise: the hooting of owls or the sudden, sharp shriek of a fox. There were rustlings, also, and other odd sounds that were hard to identify. He stuck his head out and shone his flashlight around, but the little pool of light only made the surrounding darkness blacker somehow. He was aware of the huge bulk of the house looming above him. It seemed to grow outward, radiating blackness, overshadowing, reaching toward the dim, tinny shine of the trailer. That seemed farther off now, like a toy. Suddenly, it looked very small, as if seen through the wrong end of a telescope. He could knock on the door and demand to be allowed in, but then they would know he was scared. That was not the only reason. He could not leave the tent. He was gripped by a panicky feeling – he might not make it in time. Make it from what? There was nothing out there, he told himself. It was a hot night, but he made sure to zip the flap tightly. He could make it through just one night, he thought, as he huddled down into his sleeping bag.

Things look better in daylight. In the morning, Sam didn't like to admit his fear. He moved his tent, pitching it next to the trailer, rationalising away his night terror, coming up with things Dad might say: too much imagination brought on by difference, strangeness, a change in environment.

Eddie Mayer drew up in his truck, going through the jobs for that day in his head. He scanned the brooding facade of the house. He knew all about its history. His great-grandfather had been one of the builders involved in the Edwardian renovation. He'd been a bit of a cunning man. Eddie wouldn't mind betting that he'd been responsible for the witch bottle they'd found last week. It would have been put there to protect the building from evil, and if anywhere needed protecting, this place did. Eddie had been surprised when Haslet and Jones sold it. The house had been on the market for ages, and with good reason, but then this London chap comes along. Old man Haslet had tipped him the wink, because there was a lot of work to be done, enough to keep Mayer & Son busy for months. There were plenty of stories, all right. He would not like to be here at night. Not that he'd be saying anything, and neither would his men. The new owner might take fright, and Eddie had already bought the materials and taken on extra workers. He could do without a cancelled contract.

Tom Mayer jumped down from the truck. He was tall and dark, well muscled and tanned from working with his father.

He knew the work, the business, but he was going to college, and after that he planned to get a white-collar job. He had no intention of doing this for the rest of his life. Not that he'd told his father. It would break the old man's heart. What was more to the point, he might not hand any more money out, and Tom was always short on funds. Eddie might even take away his car.

'Would you like some tea?'

Tom smiled down at the girl offering him a mug. Not very old. Fourteen? Fifteen? She'd be pretty if she wore her hair different and lost the braces. Nice eyes, though, and those shorts and crop top really showed off her figure. Things were looking up.

'Hi, I'm Tom,' he said. His smile grew wider and he crinkled his dark blue eyes.

'I'm Kate. Kate Banks.'

'Hi, Kate. You weren't here last week.'

'No. I came on the weekend with my brother. We're helping Dad. Spending the summer…'

'Bit boring for you.' Tom folded his arms and looked sympathetic. He made his mind up quickly about girls and didn't waste time. 'Tell you what. There's a barbecue tonight in the village. Want to come along – meet some people?'

'Yes,' Kate said. She was so taken aback by his invitation, she'd agreed before she'd even thought about it. 'That's if Dad says it's okay.'

'He can come. Your brother, too. It's a family thing.' Always a winner, that. He looked around. His dad was shaking a shovel and pointing at the house. 'That's me. Gotta go. Thanks for the tea. See you later.'

Kate walked away, smiling to herself. He was all right! Only been here a day and she'd gotten a date. What would the girls think about that!

Sam adjusted his facemask against the fine plaster dust billowing from the sitting room. The ground floor was being systematically stripped. The house was far older than it looked, Eddie said, and Dad was interested in uncovering some of the original building. If the theory was correct, there should be a bigger, more ancient fireplace behind the Victorian grate. All work had stopped as everyone gathered to see if Eddie was right.

'Okay. Stand back!' Eddie spat on his palms and hefted the sledgehammer.

The thick muscles bulged in his shoulders and arms as he dealt the chimney piece such a mighty crack that the whole house shook. Everyone jumped back as plaster and rubble poured across the room, sending up a great plume of dust and soot.

'Come on,' Eddie shouted, appearing like a ghost through the choking cloud. 'Get this lot shifted.'

'What the—'

The workman dropped his shovel, backing away from the thing as it bounced and skittered over the scree of plaster. The dried-up body of a cat. Tufts of black fur still mottled the brittle blue-grey skin as it lay stretched, the bone-thin back legs flexed, front paws extended, blunt head up, as if it had been set to hunt through eternity.

'Well, I'll be...' Eddie removed his mask and licked his black-rimmed lips. 'Haven't seen one of them in a while.'

'Where did it come from?' Sam asked, staring at the pathetic little corpse.

'From the chimney,' Eddie replied,

'How did it get there?'

'Dunno, son,' the builder said with a shrug. 'These old chimneys are full of nooks and crannies. Probably crawled up when the fire was out, for warmth, and died of fumes when someone lit the coals.'

It seemed a good enough explanation, but Sam could tell that he was lying by the way his eyes shifted, by the way he licked his blackberry lips.

One of the men went to shovel up the remains with the rest of the rubbish, but Eddie ordered the thing to be burned. Any protection the creature might have offered was gone now, but that was no reason to treat it with disrespect.

Eddie set to work shovelling the rubble out, while the rest of his men dispersed to work in different parts of the house. Tom had been sent upstairs to see what needed doing up there. Curiosity more than any instruction from his father took him to the little turret room at the end of the second-floor corridor. The house was haunted, so they said. This room was where it was supposed to kick off. He stepped inside and looked around. There was no physical evidence of violence and sudden death. He stood, waiting. To his intense disappointment, he felt absolutely nothing. Not even the slightest shiver. No sign at all of the psychic activity that was supposed to circulate from this very room.

He went to the window and looked out. Nice view. Kate was sunbathing on a patch of grass below. You could see even more of her figure now. He'd seen the other men looking at her...

He pressed the window frame with his thumb. The wood was soft. Rotten underneath the paint. The whole thing would have to be replaced. He blow-torched a patch of paint to find how bad it was, how far it spread. The layers bubbled back, turning from yellowy-white to brown and then black. He scraped away at the goo and put his mask up against the acrid fumes. His father was right to be strict about that – they'd used all kinds of poisons to make paint back then: lead, arsenic, you name it. His eyes strayed back to the girl and stayed on her a long time. He was finding it hard to concentrate. She shouldn't be showing herself off that way where the other men could see. It wasn't right. Her dad should have a word with her. Or he would tell her tonight... He stood there, brooding. Jealousy and anger growing within him. He shook his head, trying to clear it. He'd only just met her, and he was thinking about her as though she were his girlfriend or something. Maybe the fumes *were* getting to him. He pulled his mask tighter. It was almost as though his thoughts belonged to someone else.

He stayed only a little while longer, but by then the damage was done. No kind of mask could protect against the poison that seeped from the fabric of that particular room.

Sam had been looking forward to the barbecue, hoping to meet some kids his own age there, but most turned out to be younger, so he stayed with Dad. Sam wished he was old enough to join Kate and hang out with Tom and his friends drinking beer. That looked like more fun – although he'd be annoyed if he were Kate. Tom had seemed like a nice guy, pretty happy-go-lucky, but he obviously had another side to him. He kept her close, as if they'd been going out forever, and he didn't like it if she went away from him or talked to anyone else. She seemed okay with it. When Tom's friends moved to their cars, ready to go somewhere, she came to ask Dad if she could go with them. He said that she could, as long as she wasn't back late.

Sam didn't know how late it was, but he was woken up by a door slamming and what sounded like a sob. A car drove off, engine roar and wheel spin ripping through the silence. The trailer door opened and Dad called out, sounding anxious. Kate replied to him, and Sam heard her go in. Or at least, he thought he did.

When Sam woke again, he was dying to pee, He crawled out of the tent, urgency quelling any fears he might be feeling. He wasn't scared anymore. Moonlight made tonight quite different. It was pleasant to be outside after the stuffiness of the tent. He wandered up toward the top of the garden, looking at the stars.

That's when he saw them.

They were in the ruined summerhouse. Lit by moonlight. Two people standing close enough for their shadows to almost merge. Sam stood transfixed. One was taller, bending down toward the other. He could hear them murmuring, whispering, and then the shadows joined into just one shape. He found it hard to tear himself away. It must be Tom and Kate. Maybe they'd had a fight or something, and were getting back together. But he'd heard her go into the trailer, he was sure. How had she sneaked out again without disturbing Dad?

Not that Sam had much of a chance to find out. The next day, Kate stayed in the trailer. When Sam asked what was the matter, she refused to answer. Dad said he didn't know either, but he looked as though he wished Mom were here.

There was no sign of Tom.

'Stayed at his friend's house and hasn't turned up this morning,' Eddie said. 'If he weren't the son and heir, I'd fire him.' The builder laughed and ruffled Sam's hair. 'You'll have to do instead.'

Sam spent the morning with Eddie, but by the afternoon he had tired of the dust and noise. He mounted the stairs to get away from it. The upper floors would be deserted and quiet. He hadn't really explored up there.

Sam looked along the dark-panelled corridors leading off from the first landing and decided to take the left-hand passage, pushing doors open one by one. Most of the rooms were empty, with bare wooden floorboards and chipped skirting boards. The old furnishings showed as darker patches on the wallpaper, like ghostly imprints of the former inhabitants.

The room at the end was round, like a turret. Light shone through the open door, spilling bright into the tunnel-like passage. Sam squinted, trying to see better. There seemed to be someone in there. A girl standing at the window, facing out, away from him. She raised her arms, the light around her breaking into shafts in the dust-laden air. It was hard to see because of this halo effect, but it had to be Kate. What was she doing up here? It was the room she wanted, so perhaps she'd come to inspect it. But how did she get past him? He looked around, as if to check his route again. When he turned back, the room was empty. The girl was gone.

Sam went in cautiously, searching the room carefully, looking for a secret passage or stairway, but if there was one there, he failed to find it. He was about to go, when he noticed something. Something on the wall. He hadn't noticed it before. It was as if it had suddenly appeared. Strange. Weird. He'd have to tell Kate.

He found her in the trailer, reading a book.

'How did you do it?' he asked.

'How did I do what?' she replied without looking up.

'Get out of the room without me seeing.'

'What room? I don't know what you're talking about.'

'Yes, you do. The little turret room. I saw you up there.'

Kate looked up. 'I've been here, all afternoon reading this book.'

'Well, okay.' Sam didn't believe her, but stopped short of calling her a liar. 'But you better come. There's something you ought to see.'

'Aren't you a bit old for writing on walls?'

'It wasn't me! I swear it! It just appeared...'

The writing was a jagged scrawl, the letters at least a foot tall.

KATE
PLEASE

'And I'm supposed to think you've got nothing to do with this?' Kate turned on her brother. 'Yeah. Right!'

'Tom was up here yesterday.' Sam spoke cautiously, sensing Kate didn't want to talk about him. 'Maybe he—'

'No. Why would he?' Her tone was cold, dismissive.

The writing was malformed. There was something hideous about the straggling, spidery letters. Why would Tom do that? It was easier to believe that Sam had done it, even though he was telling the truth and Kate knew it. She grabbed a loose corner. The sheet came away, buckling to the floor. There was more underneath.

I AM TRYING

Kate worked away at the edges of the paper with her fingernails, pulling it off the wall in strips. On the layer below was more writing in the same spiked hand.

LISTEN
TO ME

'The men are leaving,' Sam said as he looked out of the window at the sound of the truck. 'It's getting late. Dad's waving us down to go into town.'

'You go. I want to get to the bottom of this.'

Kate went to find some kind of scraper and came back with a chisel and a trowel. The writing both intrigued and disturbed her. She'd thought at first that maybe it was Tom, but now words were appearing below the surface layer. She worked in the still quietness of the deserted house with single-minded intensity, seeing only the patch of paper before her. She put the curls of paper on the floor as she found them. Maybe a girl named Kate had lived here once. It was a common enough name, after all. These messages must have been left for her by some other person. That had to be the explanation. Someone who didn't write very well. A servant, maybe. Lots of people couldn't write back then. Or someone who had to use his or her other hand for some reason, perhaps because of a broken arm or something...

* * * *

Sam had not wanted to leave Kate in the house on her own, but he knew it was no use arguing.

'Where's Kate?' his dad asked.

'She doesn't want to come.'

Mark Banks shrugged, not surprised. Kate had been in a mood all day.

'I don't think we should leave her–' Sam started to say, but his dad interrupted him.

'Why not? She's a big girl now, and I don't have time to argue. I've got things to do, I want to catch the museum before it closes. They've got some news for me.'

'About what?'

'That bottle the builders found.'

Sam settled back in his seat. That sounded interesting. Some of his concern for Kate slipped from his mind as his father headed into town.

The young curator was there to meet them. She'd prepared a written report on their find. Sam craned to read it over his father's arm.

Witch bottles may be of glass or pottery and are usually found concealed beneath the hearth or threshold, but sometimes in walls or beneath the floor. Upon analysis, these bottles have most commonly been found to contain iron, in the form of pins or nails (often bent), human hair, and urine. All of these substances have associations with folk magic and together would seem to constitute a kind of spell. The locations in which these bottles were placed are significant. There is an emphasis on placing the objects at the entry and exit points of the building to serve as protection against supernatural forces that might want to invade the premises.

The curator held up their bottle, agitating it slightly.

'Your find pretty much conforms to the norm as far as contents are concerned. Have there been any more finds of a similar nature?'

'They found a dead cat yesterday,' Sam said.

'*Did* they?' The young woman turned her vivid blue eyes on him. 'Where exactly?'

'In the chimney.'

'Now *that's* interesting. The finding of dried-up cats in buildings is quite common,' she said, addressing both of them. 'Some may have died naturally, but there is ample evidence to suggest that many of these poor creatures were deliberately placed at significant points, particularly the chimney or hearth, and that they were put there as some form of protective magic. Cats were widely believed to be gifted with sixth sense and to have psychic awareness. So maybe they were put there so that they could exercise their psychic ability and hunting prowess as spiritual protectors of the house. That's what I think, anyway. Were the remains kept, by any chance?'

'No.' Mark Banks shook his head. 'Disposed of, I'm afraid.'

'Pity.' The young woman frowned. 'That's the difficulty. People don't hang on to them. Too yucky. They usually end up in the trash.' She looked up at Mark. 'I don't suppose you'd be willing to donate the bottle to the museum?'

Mark smiled, 'I'd be delighted!'

'Oh, good.' Her face cleared, and she smiled back at him. 'Where is the house, by the way?'

'Just out of Stoneham. On Amershed Road. It's set back a bit–'

'The Pearson house?'

'Why, yes.'

'Oh, that explains a lot. The house has something of a history. There's a famous ghost story attached to it. Didn't you know?'

Mark shook his head.

'What happened? In the story, I mean,' Sam asked, gripped by a creeping dread.

'Well, you know the turret room?' Sam nodded, his unease growing.

'A young girl died there in Victorian times. She was found below the window. Fell, apparently, but whether she threw herself out or someone pushed her, nobody knows. Restless spirit, though. There have been sightings ever since.'

Sam listened, a sense of terrible foreboding settling inside him, giving him a sick, cold feeling as if he'd taken down a whole mouthful of ice cream in one big swallow.

'When ... when there's a sighting,' he asked, 'what do people usually see?'

'Well, usually she's standing by the window, with her arms raised, like so.'

'Come on, Dad!' Sam grabbed his father's arm, pulling him toward the museum's glass doors.

'What's the rush?' His father looked down at him, thoroughly puzzled.

'I'll explain in the car. We have to go!'

He knew where she was. He'd seen her come to the window. He'd been watching for most of the afternoon, hidden in the trees, waiting for them all to go. Different thoughts turned and twisted in his head, braiding themselves together until he knew what he would do. He couldn't let it go. Rejecting him like that. It was too humiliating. He'd show her. And her father. A tradesman's son. She thought he wasn't good enough. Well, he'd teach her. A thin smile curled. But he'd have his satisfaction first...

Tom didn't even question how he knew the staircase was there. He just did, that was all. He found the little door to the servants' passage at the base of the tower and crept up the winding stairway, feeling his way to the room where she'd be waiting, his shuffling feet scraping on the gritty stone.

Kate rocked back on her heels, surveying the words that she had just revealed.

NOW

A WARNING

GO

What could that mean? The words were at odds with the previous messages, perhaps signifying a new twist in the tale. Speculating about the possible story behind the phenomenon took some of the strangeness from it, made it seem less sinister. She stared at the wall, so completely absorbed in her thoughts that she heard nothing. His soft-soled footfalls were almost silent. Then there was a creaking sound from the corner, a tearing crack as wood broke through paper and he was there. She leaped up, whirling around, the trowel in her hand clattering to the floor.

'How did you get there?!'

'There's more than one way up here.' Tom grinned, shutting the secret door behind him. 'I've been watching. Waiting for the others to go. For your dad and the brat to disappear. For a chance to be alone with you.' He came across the room toward her, his tone changing to harshness. 'I reckon we've got some unfinished business.'

Kate moved away from him, backing toward the window. There was nowhere else to go.

'Careful.' Tom gave a frown of feigned concern. 'The frames are rotten, and so is the stone around them.' He laughed. 'That was my job for today.'

Kate put her hand out, gripping the sill. It crumbled under her fingers like sand.

'This room's got a history. The whole house does. Didn't anyone tell you? S'pose not, or your dad never would have bought it.'

He was close now, nearly upon her. She tried to make a break across the room.

'Don't even think about it.' He grabbed her by the shoulder and pushed her back. 'A young girl died. Here. In this room. It's a tragic story. Listen to me!' The thoughts were coming thick and fast, in no particular order. 'She had a lover. They used to meet down in the summerhouse. One night she told him it was all over; she couldn't see him ever again. He followed her back here, not prepared to believe it. She wouldn't tell him why, but he guessed it. He knew her father was behind it, saying he wasn't good enough. He begged her, he pleaded, but she came across all haughty. Said she didn't love him, never had. He was a ... a dalliance. A dalliance, merely. Hardhearted little bitch she turned out to be. Needed a lesson, see? She never should have done it. Never should have rejected–' He broke off, a muscle jumping in his cheek. 'There was a fight. I don't know. Then she fell – fell from the window.' A slight shudder ran through him. He paused to collect himself. 'It doesn't have to be like that, does it? Not with you and me.'

'I – I don't know...'

Kate shrank away from him. He was really scaring her. All that must have happened a long time ago, but he was talking as though he were there. She was right up against the window now. She felt the whole frame shifting in its mountings, bulging out, the rotting frame ready to crack.

'Yes, you do. You want me as much as I want you.'

He was really close now. She could feel his breath hot on her, see his face sweating above her. She remembered how it had been in the car the night before, how hard it had been to resist him. He was so much stronger. His arms were reaching for her. She knew she wouldn't be able to fight him off a second time.

'Come on, Katie.' His voice was muffled. 'You know you want to.'

He hadn't seen the chisel hidden behind her back. The blade was thin, the wedge-shaped tip razor sharp.

Then there was noise, her name being called. Light feet running, followed by a heavier, adult tread.

'Sam! Wait!' Her father's voice was shouting. 'Leave it to me.' He was right outside now. The door was opening, 'Kate? Katie?'

Mark Banks found his daughter sitting under the window, the chisel still clutched in her hand. Tom Mayer's body lay stretched out beside her. Curls and shreds of wallpaper lay drifted about them, rustling like leaves on the bloodstained floor.

The Ghost in the Bride's Chamber
Charles Dickens

The house was a genuine old house of a very quaint description, teeming with old carvings, and beams, and panels, and having an excellent old staircase, with a gallery or upper staircase, cut off from it by a curious fence-work of old oak, or of the old Honduras Mahogany wood. It was, and is, and will be, for many a long year to come, a remarkably picturesque house; and a certain grave mystery lurking in the depth of the old mahogany panels, as if they were so many deep pools of dark water – such, indeed, as they had been much among when they were trees – gave it a very mysterious character after nightfall.

When Mr Goodchild and Mr Idle had first alighted at the door, and stepped into the sombre handsome old hall, they had been received by half a dozen noiseless old men in black, all dressed exactly alike, who glided up the stairs with the obliging landlord and waiter – but without appearing to get into their way, or to mind whether they did or no – and who had filed off to the right and left on the old staircase, as the guests entered their sitting-room. It was then broad, bright day. But, Mr Goodchild had said, when their door was shut, 'Who on earth are those old men?' And afterwards, both on going out and coming in, he had noticed that there were no old men to be seen.

Neither had the old men, or any one of the old men reappeared since. The two friends had passed a night in the house, but had seen nothing more of the old men. Mr Goodchild, in rambling about it, had looked along passages, and glanced in at doorways, but had encountered no old men; neither did it appear that any old men were, by any member of the establishment, missed or expected.

Another odd circumstance impressed itself on their attention. It was that the door of their sitting-room was never left untouched for a quarter of an hour. It was opened with hesitation, opened with confidence, opened a little way, opened a good way, always clapped-to again without a word of explanation. They were reading, they were writing, they were eating, they were drinking, they were talking, they were dozing; the door was always opened at an unexpected moment, and they looked towards it, and it was clapped-to again, and nobody was to be seen. When this had happened fifty times or so, Mr Goodchild had said to his companion, jestingly: 'I begin to think, Tom, there was something wrong with those six old men.'

Night had come again, and they had been writing for two or three hours: writing, in short, a portion of the lazy notes from which these lazy sheets are taken. They had left off writing, and glasses were on the table between them. The house was closed and quiet. Around the head of Thomas Idle, as he lay upon his sofa, hovered light wreaths of fragrant smoke. The temples of Francis Goodchild, as he leaned back in his chair, with his two hands clasped behind his head, and his legs crossed, were similarly decorated.

They had been discussing several idle subjects of speculation, not omitting the strange old men, and were still so occupied, when Mr Goodchild abruptly changed his attitude to wind up his watch. They were just becoming drowsy enough to be stopped in their talk by any such slight check. Thomas Idle, who was speaking at the moment paused and said, 'How goes it?'

'One,' said Goodchild.

As if he had ordered one old man, and the order were promptly executed (truly, all orders were so, in that excellent hotel), the door opened, and one old man stood there.

He did not come in, but stood with the door in his hand.

'One of the six, Tom, at last!' said Mr Goodchild, in a surprised whisper. 'Sir, your pleasure?'

'Sir, *your* pleasure?' said the one old man.

'I didn't ring.'

'The bell did,' said the one old man.

He said *bell,* in a deep strong way, that would have expressed the church bell.

'I had the pleasure, I believe, of seeing you yesterday?' said Goodchild.

'I cannot undertake to say for certain,' was the grim reply of the one old man.

'I think you saw me? Did you not?'

'Saw you?' said the old man. 'Oh yes, I saw you. But I see many who never see me.'

A chilled, slow, earthy, fixed old man. A cadaverous old man of measured speech. An old man who seemed as unable to wink as if his eyelids had been nailed to his forehead. An old man whose eyes – two spots of fire – had no more motion than if they had been connected with the back of his skull by screws driven through it, and riveted and bolted outside, among his grey hairs.

The night had turned so cold, to Mr Goodchild's sensations, that he shivered. He remarked lightly, and half apologetically, 'I think somebody is walking over my grave.'

'No,' said the weird old man, 'there is no one there.'

Mr Goodchild looked at Idle, but Idle lay with his head enwreathed in smoke.

'No one there?' said Goodchild.

'There is no one at your grave, I assure you,' said the old man.

He had come in and shut the door and he now sat down. He did not bend himself to sit as other people do, but seemed to sink bolt upright, as if in water, until the chair stopped him.

'My friend, Mr Idle,' said Goodchild, extremely anxious to introduce a third person into the conversation

'I am,' said the old man, without looking at him, 'at Mr Idle's service.'

'If you are an old inhabitant of this place –' Francis Goodchild resumed –

'Yes.'

'Perhaps you can decide a point my friend and I were in doubt upon, this morning. They hang condemned criminals at the castle, I believe?'

'*I* believe so,' said the old man.

'Are their faces turned towards that noble prospect?'

'Your face is turned,' replied the old man, 'to the castle wall. When you are tied up, you see its stones expanding and contracting violently, and a similar expansion and contraction seem to take place in your own head and breast. Then, there is a rush of fire and an earthquake, and the castle springs into the air, and you tumble down a precipice.'

His cravat seemed to trouble him. He put his hand to his throat, and moved his neck from side to side. He was an old man of a swollen character of face, and his nose was immovably hitched upon one side, as if by a little hook inserted in that nostril. Mr Goodchild felt exceedingly uncomfortable, and began to think the night was hot, and not cold.

'A strong description, sir,' he observed.

'A strong sensation,' the old man rejoined.

Again, Mr Goodchild looked to Mr Thomas Idle; but Thomas lay on his back with his face attentively turned towards the one old man, and made no sign. At this time Mr Goodchild believed that he saw threads of fire stretch from the old man's eyes to his own, and there attach themselves. (Mr Goodchild writes the present account of his experience, and, with the utmost solemnity, protests that he had the strongest sensation upon him of being forced to look at the old man along those two fiery films, from that moment.)

'I must tell it to you,' said the old man, with a ghastly and a stony stare.

'What?' asked Francis Goodchild.

'You know where it took place. Yonder!'

Whether he pointed to the room above, or to the room below, or to any room in that old house, or to a room in some other old house in that old town, Mr Goodchild was not, nor is, nor ever can be, sure. He was confused by the circumstances that the right forefinger of the one old man seemed to dip itself in one of the threads of fire, light itself, and make a fiery start in the air, as it pointed somewhere. Having pointed somewhere, it went out.

'You know she was a bride,' said the old man.

'I know they still send up bride-cake,' Mr Goodchild faltered. 'This is a very oppressive air.'

'She was a bride,' said the old man. 'She was a fair, flaxen-haired, large-eyed girl, who had no character, no purpose. A weak, credulous, incapable, helpless nothing. Not like her mother. No, no. It was her father whose character she reflected.

'Her mother had taken care to secure everything to herself, for her own life, when the father of this girl (a child at that time) died – of sheer helplessness; no other disorder – and then HE renewed the acquaintance that had once subsisted between the mother and him. He had been put aside for the flaxen-haired, large-eyed man (or nonentity) with money. He could overlook that for money. He wanted compensation in money.

'So, he returned to the side of that woman the mother, made love to her again, danced attendance on her, and submitted himself to her whims. She wreaked upon him every whim she had, or could invent. He bore it. And the more he bore, the more he wanted compensation in money, and the more he was resolved to have it.

'But lo! Before he got it, she cheated him. In one of her imperious states, she froze, and never thawed again. She put her hands to her head one night, uttered a cry, stiffened, lay in that attitude certain hours, and died. Again he had got no compensation from her in money, yet. Blight and murrain on her! Not a penny.

'He had hated her throughout that second pursuit, and had longed for retaliation on her. He now counterfeited her signature to an instrument, leaving all she had to leave to her daughter – ten years old then – to whom the property passed absolutely, and appointed himself the daughter's guardian. When he slid it under the pillow of the bed on which she lay, he bent down in the deaf ear of death, and whispered: "Mistress Pride, I have determined a long time that, dead or alive, you must make me compensation in money."

'So, now there were only two left. Which two were HE and the fair flaxen-haired, large-eyed foolish daughter, who afterwards became the bride.

'He put her to school. In a secret, dark, oppressive, ancient house, he put her to school with a watchful and unscrupulous woman. "My worthy lady," he said, "here is a mind to be formed; will you help me to form it?" She accepted the trust. For which she, too, wanted compensation in money, and had it.

'The girl was formed in the fear of him, and in the conviction, that there was no escape from him. She was taught, from the first, to regard him as her future husband – the man who must marry her – the destiny that overshadowed her – the appointed certainty that could never be evaded. The poor fool was soft white wax in their hands, and took the impression that they put upon her. It hardened with time. It became a part of herself.

Inseparable from herself and only to be torn away from her by tearing life away from her.

'Eleven years she had lived in the dark house and its gloomy garden. He was jealous of the very light and air getting to her, and they kept her close. He stopped the wide chimneys, shaded the little windows, left the strong-stemmed ivy to wander where it would over the house-front, the moss to accumulate on the untrimmed fruit trees in the red-walled garden, the weeds to over-run its green and yellow walks. He surrounded her with images of sorrow and desolation. He caused her to be filled with fears of the place and of the stories that were told of it, and then on pretext of correcting them, to be left in it in solitude, or made to shrink about it in the dark. When her mind was most depressed and fullest of terrors, then he would come out of one of the hiding-places from which he overlooked her and present himself as her sole recourse.

'Thus, by being from her childhood the one embodiment her life presented to her of power to coerce and power to relieve, power to bind and power to loose, the ascendency over her weakness was secured. She was twenty-one years and twenty-one days old when he brought her home to the gloomy house, his half-witted, frightened, and submissive bride of three weeks.

'He had dismissed the governess by that time – what he had left to do, he could best do alone – and they came back, upon a rainy night, to the scene of her long preparation.

'She turned to him upon the threshold, as the rain was dripping from the porch, and said: "Oh sir, it is the death-watch ticking for me!"

'"Well!" he answered. "And if it were?"

'"Oh sir!" she returned to him, "look kindly on me, and be merciful to me! I beg your pardon. I will do anything you wish, if you will only forgive me!"

'That had become the poor fool's constant song: "I beg your pardon," and "Forgive me!"

'She was not worth hating; he felt nothing but contempt for her. But she had long been in the way, and he had long been weary, and the work was near its end, and had to be worked out.

'"You fool," he said. "Go up the stairs!"

'She obeyed very quickly, murmuring, "I will do anything you wish!" When he came into the bride's chamber, having been a little retarded by the heavy fastenings of the great door (for they were alone in the house, and he had arranged that the people who attended on them should come and go in the day), he found her withdrawn to the furthest corner, and there standing pressed against the panelling as if she would have shrunk through it: her flaxen hair all wild about her face, and her large eyes staring at him in vague terror.

'"What are you afraid of? Come and sit down by me."

'"I will do anything you wish. I beg your pardon, sir. Forgive me!" Her monotonous tune as usual.

'"Ellen, here is a writing that you must write out tomorrow, in your own hand. You may as well be seen by others, busily engaged upon it. When you have written it all fairly, and corrected all mistakes, call in any two people there may be about the house, and sign your name to it before them. Then, put it in your bosom to keep it safe, and when I sit here again tomorrow night, give it to me."

'"I will do it all, with the greatest care. I will do anything you wish."

'"Don't shake and tremble, then."

'"I will try my utmost not to do it – if you will only forgive me!"

'Next day, she sat down at her desk, and did as she had been told. He often passed in and out of the room, to observe her, and always saw her slowly and laboriously writing: repeating to herself the words she copied, in appearance quite mechanically, and without caring or endeavouring to comprehend them, so that she did her task. He saw her follow the directions she had received, in all particulars; and at night, when they were alone again in the same bride's chamber, and he drew his chair to the hearth, she timidly approached him from her distant seat, took the paper from her bosom, and gave it into his hand.

'It secured all her possessions to him, in the event of her death. He put her before him, face to face, that he might look at her steadily; and he asked her, in so many plain words, neither fewer nor more, did she know that?

'There were spots of ink upon the bosom of her white dress, and they made her face look whiter and her eyes look larger as she nodded her head. There were spots of ink upon the hand with which she stood before him nervously plaiting and folding her white skirts.

'He took her by the arm, and looked her, yet more closely and steadily, in the face. "Now, die! I have done with you."

'She shrank, and uttered a low, suppressed cry.

'"I am not going to kill you. I will not endanger my life for yours. Die!"

'He sat before her in the gloomy bride's chamber, day after day, night after night, looking the word at her when he did not utter it. As often as her large unmeaning eyes were raised from the hands in which she rocked her head to the stern figure sitting with crossed arms and knitted forehead in the chair, they read in it, "Die!" When she dropped asleep in exhaustion, she was called back to shuddering consciousness by the whisper, "Die!" When she fell upon her old entreaty to be pardoned, she was answered, "Die!" When she had out-watched and out-suffered the long night, and the rising sun flamed into the sombre room, she heard it hailed with, "Another day and not dead?"

'It was done, upon a windy morning, before sunrise. He computed the time to be half-past four; but his forgotten watch had run down and he could not be sure. She had broken away from him in the night with loud and sudden cries – the first of that kind to which she had given vent – and he had had to put his hands over her mouth. Since then, she had been quiet in the corner of the panelling where she had sunk down; and he had left her and had gone back with his folded arms and his knitted forehead to his chair.

'Paler in the pale light, more colourless than ever in the leaden dawn, he saw her coming, trailing herself along the floor towards him – a white wreck of hair, and dress, and wild eyes, pushing itself on by an irresolute and bending hand.

'"Oh, forgive me! I will do anything. Oh, sir, pray tell me I may live!"

'"Die!"

'"Are you so resolved? Is there no hope for me?"

'"Die!"

'Her large eyes strained themselves with wonder and fear; wonder and fear changed to reproach; reproach to blank nothing. It was done. He was not at first so sure it was done, but that the morning sun was hanging jewels in her hair – he saw the diamond, emerald and ruby, glittering among it in little points, as he stood looking down at her – when he lifted her and laid her on her bed.

'She was soon laid in the ground. And now they were all gone, and he had compensated himself well.

'He had a mind to travel. Not that he meant to waste his money, for he was a pinching man and liked his money dearly (like nothing else, indeed), but that he had grown tired of the desolate house and wished to turn his back upon it and have done with it. But, the house was worth money, and money must not be thrown away. He determined to sell it before he went. That it might look the less wretched and bring a better price, he hired some labourers to work in the overgrown garden: to cut out the dead wood, trim the ivy that dropped in heavy masses over the windows and gables, and clear the walks in which the weeds were growing mid-leg high.

'He worked, himself, along with them. He worked later than they did, and, one evening at dusk, was left working alone with his billhook in his hand. One autumn evening, when the bride was five weeks dead,

'"It grows too dark to work longer," he said to himself. "I must give over for the night."

'He detested the house, and was loath to enter it. He looked at the dark porch waiting for him like a tomb, and felt that it was an accursed house. Near to the porch, and near to where he stood, was a tree whose branches waved before the old bay window of the bride's chamber, where it had been done. The tree swung suddenly, and made him start. It swung again, although the night was still. Looking up into it, he saw a figure among the branches.

'It was the figure of a young man. The face looked down, as he looked up; the branches cracked and swayed; the figure rapidly descended, and slid upon its feet before him. A slender youth of about her age, with long light brown hair.

'"What thief are you?" he said, seizing the youth by the collar.

'The young man, in shaking himself free, swung him a blow with his arm across the face and throat. They closed, but the young man got from him and stepped back, crying, with great eagerness and horror, "Don't touch me! I would as lieve be touched by the devil!"

'He stood still, with his billhook in his hand, looking at the young man. For the young man's look was the counterpart of her last look, and he had not expected ever to see that again.

'"I am no thief. Even if I were, I would not have a coin of your wealth, if it would buy me the Indies. You murderer!"

'"What!"

'"I climbed it," said the young man, pointing up into the tree, "for the first time, nigh four years ago. I climbed it, to look at her. I saw her. I spoke to her. I have climbed it, many a time, to watch and listen for her. I was a boy, hidden among its leaves, when from that bay window she gave me this!"

'He showed a tress of flaxen hair, tied with a mourning ribbon.

'"Her life," said the young man, "was a life of mourning. She gave me this, as a token of it, and a sign that she was dead to everyone but you. If I had been older, if I had seen her sooner, I might have saved her from you. But she was fast in the web when I first climbed the tree, and what could I do then to break it!"

'In saying these words, he burst into a fit of sobbing and crying: weakly at first, then passionately.

'"Murderer! I climbed the tree on the night when you brought her back. I heard her, from the tree, speak of the death-watch at the door. I was three times in the tree while you were shut up with her, slowly killing her. I saw her, from the tree, lie dead upon her bed. I have watched you, from the tree, for proofs and traces of your guilt. The manner of it is a mystery to me yet, but I will pursue you until you have rendered up your life to the hangman. You shall never, until then, be rid of me. I loved her! I can know no relenting towards you. Murderer! I loved her!"

'The youth was bareheaded, his hat having fluttered away in his descent from the tree. He moved towards the gate. He had to pass − HIM − to get to it. There was breadth for two old-fashioned carriages abreast; and the youth's abhorrence, openly expressed in every feature of his face and limb of his body, and very hard to bear, had verge enough to keep itself at a distance in. He (by which I mean the other) had not stirred hand or feet since he had stood still to look at the boy. He faced round, now, to follow him with his eyes. As the back of the bare light-brown head was turned to him, he saw a red curve stretch from his hand to it. He knew, before he threw the billhook, where it had alighted – I say, had alighted, and not, would alight; for, to his clear perception the thing was done before he did it. It cleft the head, and it remained there, and the boy lay on his face.

'He buried the body in the night, at the foot of the tree. As soon as it was light in the morning, he worked at turning up all the ground near the tree, and hacking and hewing at the neighbouring bushes and undergrowth. When the labourers came, there was nothing suspicious, and nothing suspected.

'But, he had, in a moment, defeated all his precautions, and destroyed the triumph of the scheme he had so long concerted, and so successfully worked out. He had got rid of the bride, and had acquired her fortune without endangering his life; but now, for a death by which he had gained nothing, he had evermore to live with a rope around his neck.

'Beyond this, he was chained to the house of gloom and horror, which he could not endure. Being afraid to sell it or to quit it, lest discovery should be made, he was forced to live in it. He hired two old people, man and wife, for his servants; and dwelt in it, and dreaded it. His great difficulty, for a long time, was the garden. Whether he should keep it trim, whether he should suffer it to fall into its former state of neglect, what would be the least likely way of attracting attention to it?

'He took the middle course of gardening, himself, in his evening leisure, and of then calling the old serving-man to help him; but, of never letting him work there alone. And he made himself an arbour over against the tree, where he could sit and see that it was safe.

'As the seasons changed, and the tree changed, his mind perceived dangers that were always changing. In the leafy time, he perceived that the upper boughs were growing into the form of the young man – that they made the shape of him exactly, sitting in a forked branch swinging in the wind. In the time of the falling leaves he perceived that they came down from the tree, forming tell-tale letters on the path, or that they had a tendency to heap themselves into a churchyard mound above the grave. In the winter, when the tree was bare, he perceived that the boughs swung at him the ghost of the blow the young man had given, and that they threatened him openly. In the spring, when sap was mounting in the trunk, he asked himself, were the dried-up particles of blood mounting with it – to make out, more obviously this year than last, the leaf-screened figure of the young man, swinging in the wind?

'However, he turned his money over and over, and still over. He was in the dark trade, the gold-dust trade, and most secret trades that yielded great returns. In ten years, he had turned his money over so many times that the traders and shippers who had dealings with him absolutely did not lie – for once – when they declared that he had increased his fortune twelve hundred per cent.

'He possessed his riches one hundred years ago, when people could be lost easily. He had heard who the youth was, from hearing of the search that was made after him; but, it died away, and the youth was forgotten.

'The annual round of changes in the tree had been repeated ten times since the night of the burial at its foot, when there was a great thunderstorm over this place. It broke at midnight, and raged until morning. The first intelligence he heard from his old serving-man that morning was that the tree had been struck by lightning.

'It had been riven down the stem, in a very surprising manner and the stem lay in two blighted shafts: one resting against the house, and one against a portion of the old red garden-wall in which its fall had made a gap. The fissure went down the tree to a little above the earth, and there stopped. There was great curiosity to see the tree, and, with most of his former fears revived, he sat in his arbour – grown quite an old man – watching the people who came to see it.

'They quickly began to come, in such dangerous numbers that he closed his garden-gate and refused to admit any more. But there were certain men of science who travelled from a distance to examine the tree, and, in an evil hour, he let them in – blight and murrain on them, let them in!

'They wanted to dig up the ruin by the roots, and closely examine it, and the earth about it. Never, while he lived! They offered money for it. They! Men of science, whom he could have bought by the gross, with a scratch of his pen! He showed them the garden gate again, and locked and barred it.

'But they were bent on doing what they wanted to do, and they bribed the old serving-man – a thankless wretch who regularly complained, when he received his wages, of being underpaid – and they stole into the garden by night with their lanterns, picks, and shovels, and fell to at the tree. He was lying in a turret room on the other side of the house (the bride's chamber had been unoccupied ever since), but he soon dreamed of picks and shovels, and got up.

'He came to an upper window on that side, whence he could see their lanterns, and them, and the loose earth in a heap which he had himself disturbed and put back when it was last turned to the air. It was found. They had that minute lighted on it. They were all bending over it. One of them said, "The skull is fractured"; and another, "See here the bones"; said another, "See here the clothes"; and then the first struck in again, and said, "A rusty billhook!"

'He became sensible, next day, that he was already put under a strict watch, and that he could go nowhere without being followed. Before a week was out he was taken and laid in hold. The circumstances were gradually pieced together against him, with a desperate malignity, and an appalling ingenuity. But, see the justice of men and how it was extended to him! He was further accused of having poisoned that girl in the bride's chamber. He, who had carefully and expressly avoided imperilling a hair of his head for her, and who had seen her die of her own incapacity.

'There was doubt for which of the two murders he should be first tried; but, the real one was chosen, and he was found guilty, and cast for death. Bloodthirsty wretches! They would have made him guilty of anything, so set they were upon having his life.

'His money could do nothing to save him, and he was hanged. *I* am he, and I was hanged at Lancaster Castle, with my face to the wall, a hundred years ago!'

At this terrific announcement, Mr Goodchild tried to rise and cry out. But, the two fiery lines extending from the old man's eyes to his own, kept him down, and he could not utter a sound, His sense of hearing, however, was acute, and he could hear the clock strike two. No sooner had he heard the clock strike two, than he saw before him two old men!

Two.

The eyes of each, connected with his eyes by two films of fire: each, exactly like the other; each, addressing him at precisely one and the same instant; each, gnashing the same teeth in the same head, with the same twitched nostril above them, and the same suffused expression around it. Two old men. Differing in nothing, equally distinct to the sight, the copy no fainter than the original, the second as real as the first.

'At what time,' said the two old men, 'did you arrive at the door below?'

'At six.'

'And there were six old men upon the stairs!'

Mr Goodchild having wiped the perspiration from his brow, or tried to do it, the two old men proceeded in one voice, and in the singular number:

'I had been anatomised, but had not yet had my skeleton put together and re-hung on an iron hook, when it began to be whispered that the bride's chamber was haunted. It *was* haunted, and I was there.

'*We* were there. She and I were there. I, in the chair upon the hearth; she, a white wreck again, trailing itself towards me on the floor. But, I was the speaker no more, and the one word that she said to me from midnight until dawn was, "Live!"

'The youth was there, likewise. In the tree outside the window. Coming and going in the moonlight, as the tree bent and gave. He has, ever since, been there, peeping in at me in my torment; revealing to me by snatches, in the pale light and slatey shadows, where he comes and goes, bareheaded – a billhook standing edgewise in his hair.

'In the bride's chamber, every night from midnight until dawn – one month in the year excepted, as I am going to tell you – he hides in the tree, and she comes towards me on the floor; always approaching; never coming nearer; always visible as if by moonlight, whether the moon shines or no; always saying, from midnight until dawn, her one word, "Live!"

'But, in the month wherein I was forced out of this life – this present month of thirty days – the bride's chamber is empty and quiet. Not so my old dungeon. Not so the rooms where I was restless and afraid, ten years. Both are fitfully haunted then. At one in the morning, I am what you saw me when the clock struck that hour – one old man. At two in the morning, I am two old men. At three, I am three. By twelve noon, I am twelve old men. One for every hundred per cent of old gain. Every one of the twelve, with twelve times my old power of suffering and agony. From that hour until twelve at night, I, twelve old men in anguish and fearful forebodings, wait for the coming of the executioner. At twelve at night, I, twelve old men turned off, swing invisible outside Lancaster Castle, with twelve faces to the wall!

'When the bride's chamber was first haunted, it was known to me that this punishment would never cease until I could make its nature, and my story, known to two living men together. I waited for the coming of two living men together into the bride's chamber, years upon years. It was infused into my knowledge (of the means I am ignorant) that if two living men, with their eyes open, could be in the bride's chamber at one in the morning, they would see me sitting in my chair.

'At length, the whispers that the room was spiritually troubled, brought two men to try the adventure. I was scarcely struck upon the hearth at midnight (I come there as if the lightning blasted me into being), when I heard them ascending the stairs. Next, I saw them enter. One of them was a bold, gay, active man, in the prime of life, some five and forty years of age; the other, a dozen years younger. They brought provisions with them in a basket, and bottles. A young woman accompanied them, with wood and coals for the lighting of the fire. When he had lighted it, the bold, gay, active man accompanied her along the gallery outside the room, to see her safely down the staircase, and came back laughing.

'He locked the door, examined the chamber, put out the contents of the basket on the table before the fire – little **recking** of me, in my appointed station on the hearth close to him – and filled the glasses, and ate and drank. His companion did the same, and was as cheerful and confident as he: though he was the leader. When they had supped, they laid pistols on the table, turned to the fire, and began to smoke their pipes of foreign make.

'They had travelled together, and had been much together, and had an abundance of subjects in common. In the midst of their talking and laughing, the younger man made a reference to the leader's being always ready for any adventure; that one, or any other.

'He replied in these words: "Not quite so, Dick; if I am afraid of nothing else, I am afraid of myself."

'His companion, who seemed to grow a little dull, asked him in what sense? How?

'"Why, thus," he returned. "Here is a ghost to be disproved. Well! I cannot answer for what my fancy might do if I were alone here, or what tricks my senses might play with me if they had me to themselves. But, in company with another man, and especially with you, Dick, I would consent to out-face all the ghosts that were ever told of in the universe."

'"I had not the vanity to suppose that I was of so much importance tonight," said the other.

'"Of so much," rejoined the leader, more seriously than he had spoken yet, "that I would, for the reason I have given, on no account have undertaken to pass the night here alone."

'It was within a few minutes of one. The head of the younger man had drooped when he made his last remark, and it drooped lower now.

---

recking taking notice

' "Keep awake, Dick!" said the leader, gaily. "The small hours are the worst."

He tried, but his head drooped again.

' "Dick!" urged the leader. "Keep awake!"

' "I can't," he indistinctly muttered. "I don't know what strange influence is stealing over me. I can't."

'His companion looked at him with a sudden horror, and I, in my different way, felt a new horror also; it was on the stroke of one, and I felt that the second watcher was yielding to me, and that the curse was upon me that I must send him to sleep.

' "Get up and walk, Dick!" cried the leader. "Try!"

'It was in vain to go behind the slumberer's chair and shake him. One o'clock sounded, and I was present to the elder man, and he stood transfixed before me.

'To him alone, I was obliged to relate my story, without hope of benefit. To him alone, I was an awful phantom making a quite useless confession. I foresee it will ever be the same. The two living men together will never come to release me. When I appear, the senses of one of the two will be locked in sleep; he will neither see nor hear me; my communication will ever be made to a solitary listener, and will ever be unserviceable. Woe! Woe! Woe!'

As the two old men, with these words, wrung their hands, it shot into Mr Goodchild's mind that he was in the terrible situation of being virtually alone with the spectre, and that Mr Idle's immovability was explained by his having been charmed asleep at one o'clock. In the terror of this sudden discovery which produced an indescribable dread, he struggled so hard to get free from the four fiery threads, that he snapped them, after he had pulled them out to a great width. Being then out of bonds, he caught up Mr Idle from the sofa and rushed downstairs with him.

Chicken
Mary Hoffman

It was hard to say when the group became a gang. Perhaps it was when Mark Mason tried to hang around with us and we froze him out. Or perhaps when we started calling ourselves The Inliners. Definitely we were a gang by the time of the leadership struggle or there wouldn't have been a struggle to start with. And we'd never have been so stupid as to do the dares.

We had all known each other since Nursery. Alfie and I had hung out together since before we were born actually, because our mums were best friends and they'd gone into the hospital to have us on the same day.

Dylan, Jamal and Leon all live within a couple of streets of Alfie and me. (I'm Rick, by the way.) We all learnt to swim together in the local kiddie pool, all went to birthday parties at each other's houses dressed as Power Rangers or Ninja turtles, all went up to the Juniors at the same time, all played football on the common, all went to Woodcraft and went camping together, all got our first inline skates the same Christmas.

So had a lot of other kids, of course, but our group had been special from the beginning, enjoying in-jokes and making up a sort of private language that kept our other friends at a slight distance. We were all among the oldest and biggest in our year, because we all had birthdays close to one another in September. Maybe that made us look more like a gang, like hard men. But there was nothing about us to worry our parents or our teachers until – we got into Year 6.

For the first time in our lives we were facing being split up. Alfie's parents were thinking of moving and Dylan's were putting him in for the Grammar School. Only me, Jamal and Leon were sure of being in the same secondary school and it made the whole group edgy. Maybe that's when we became a gang.

It was late October when the dares started. I suppose it was my fault really. We were just mucking about when I dared Alfie to steal some fireworks from Patel's. That's when Alfie should have said no and the whole thing would have stopped before it started. Then maybe *it* would never have happened. But he didn't.

It was pathetically easy. Mr Patel is a nice trusting man whose daughter Sushila is in our class. Alfie managed to smuggle two Skyburst rockets out under his blazer while rest of us chatted to Mr Patel about the local football team.

Later, when we set the rockets off on the common, everyone was a bit hyper. Maybe that's when the rivalry between Alfie and Dylan started. Alfie was capering round like a mad thing, the bright explosion of coloured light from the rocket dyeing his face green and purple.

'One Alfie Spencer, there's only one Alfie Spencer,' he was chanting.

'Knock it off!' grunted Dylan. 'It was only a bit of shoplifting.'

'Yeah, well,' said Alfie. 'But look who didn't do it.'

'No one asked me to,' said Dylan indignantly. 'I would've done it if it was my dare.'

'Yeah,' said Alfie.

'Go on then,' said Dylan. 'Dare me and I'll show you.'

'Yeah, dare him, Alf,' said Jamal.

Alfie thought for a minute. Not shoplifting again; that was too easy.

'Okay, Dyl,' he said slowly. 'I dare you to get Old Knickers trick or treating.'

'Old Knickers' was Mrs Nixon, our headteacher. By common consent, her house was always avoided by trick or treat gangs at Hallowe'en. Mrs Nixon had strong views on what she called 'hooliganism'. And she made them very clear in assembly on November 1st.

'Much as I dislike that American import of tolerated blackmail called Trick or Treating,' she told the whole school assembly, 'I thought there were at least some rules to it. I thought children were supposed to ask which you'd prefer. Indeed I even had a bowl of fun-size chocolate bars ready by the door...'

Jamal and Leon turned to look at me. We had missed a trick there. Or rather a treat.

'But no one rang the bell,' continued Mrs Nixon, 'and this morning I discovered my car had been decorated with pink silly string and my garden hedge was festooned with loo paper.' She glared at us and Dylan stared straight ahead.

'Lame,' whispered Alfie out of the corner of his mouth.

And so it continued all term. There was the guy of Old Knickers that was burnt at the bonfire party. That was Jamal's dare. The kidnap of Cooper, who was the ginger cat belonging to our form teacher, Miss Jellicoe. That was Leon's, only he got caught, because he was covered in scratches. He wouldn't have hurt Cooper; Leon was soppy about all animals. He was supposed to have sent a ransom note for £20, but Cooper escaped and ran home.

Then there was the fire in a wastepaper basket, which set off the smoke alarms and called out the fire brigade. That was mine, I'm now ashamed to say, and it earned me a lot of admiration in the gang.

But the main rivalry was still between Alfie and Dylan. It got worse by the end of term, when Dylan sat the exam for the Grammar School. It seemed as if Alfie was determined to take him down a peg or two.

The Inliners were beginning to split into two. I could feel it happening and I didn't like it. I always backed Alfie, of course, and Jamal tended to support Dylan. Leon was the most easy-going of all of us, and refused to take sides.

And now our parents were getting really concerned. Leon's had been horrified about the cat incident but he had managed to persuade them that it was just a practical joke gone wrong. The school had begun to suspect us because all the incidents were connected with our form and, being big and bad-looking, as I say, the suspicion naturally fell on us, even though we'd never done anything like this before.

Then Alfie twisted his ankle quite badly trying to abseil down the school wall. I have to admit that I was helping him, but I wasn't the one who had dared him to do it. All the dares now seemed to be between him and Dylan and they were getting worse. Alfie's parents asked a lot of awkward questions about what we'd been up to after dark that made him hurt his ankle, but at least no one saw us.

Then Dylan got horribly drunk doing the dare about having one glass of everything in his parents' drinks cabinet. His sick note said he had a tummy upset, but that was putting it mildly. I overheard my mum telling Alfie's it was alcohol poisoning and Dylan had had to go to hospital.

I tried to get Alfie to stop then, because it was clearly becoming dangerous, but he said it was Dylan's turn to dare him to do something next and he couldn't stop it because Dylan would call him chicken. Dylan came back to school looking very white and shaky and I saw him give Alfie an evil look at break-time. It was hard to believe that they had ever been friends.

And yet we were still all in the gang. Inliners for ever! We were all skating along the High Street together when Dylan said to Alfie, 'I dare you to take on the Terminator.'

If we hadn't been going downhill, I would have stopped. The Terminator was a boy at the comprehensive, about fourteen years old and already built like Arnie. He was Mark Mason's older brother, Tony, but everyone called him the Terminator and he liked it. Actually I don't know that he ever did anyone any damage, but he was well over six feet tall and made of solid muscle. No one had ever tried to bully Mark, let's put it that way. Alfie wouldn't stand a chance against him and Dylan knew it.

I sped up and came level with Alfie. He was looking almost as green as he had that night by the light of the stolen rockets.

'Are you mad?' I hissed. 'You're not really going to do it? You'll end up as dogmeat. I might as well call the ambulance now.'

'What's the matter, Alf?' taunted Dylan, whizzing past. 'Are you chicken?'

Alfie straightened his back and concentrated on weaving in and out of the shoppers. I could see he was going to do it.

He didn't let me in on the plan this time, so I couldn't even be around to help him when the massacre took place. I never knew what exactly happened, but a couple of days later there was a ring at my doorbell, and Alfie fell on the doormat. He looked terrible. He had a black eye, which was closing up fast, and a thick lip and blood all down his cheek.

'I did it, Rick,' he gasped, rolling over and clutching his stomach.

'I'll ring the hospital,' I said.

'No, don't,' whispered Alfie. 'Let me stay here. My parents'll kill me if they find out. Specially so soon after the ankle thing.'

'How do you think they're not going to find out, with you looking like that?' I demanded.

Fortunately the matter was taken out of our hands, because my mum came out and saw him, And that was that. She rang Alfie's mum and then drove him straight to Casualty. I was allowed to come too and Alfie's mum met us there. The grown-ups were white-faced and quiet in that way that's so much more scary than shouting.

Alfie refused to say who had done it. He had no broken bones, thank goodness, only bruising. But all hell was let loose just the same. Old Knickers had a field day in assembly, going on about bullying, and the whole gang was put on report – which was very unfair, seeing as we hadn't done anything to Alfie. Except for Dylan of course.

I honestly thought it would end there, as soon as Dylan saw Alfie's face. He looked a bit peculiar, as if he might throw up. And if Alfie had been prepared to give it up, it might have all stopped before the worst happened. But Alfie had just been given the pounding of his life, and he wasn't about to let Dylan off the hook.

Nothing happened for a week and it was nearly the end of term. I was beginning to breathe more easily. Alfie was a bit more quiet than usual but that was understandable. Then one day at break he took me to one side and said, 'Saturday afternoon, Silbury cuttings.'

My blood ran cold. I've often seen that written down, but that's actually what it feels like. As if icy water is being pumped through your veins. Silbury cuttings used to be notorious in our neighbourhood. A few years ago, a kid was killed on the railway line at Silbury cuttings. It was a result of a game of 'chicken' with the trains. Ever since then, it has been the biggest no-go area around. The number of lectures we've had in assembly about it, with the police as well, and the number of times our parents have spoken to us about it in their most serious voices – well, I just can't tell you how it made me feel to hear Alfie even mention it.

'You're kidding, right?' I said, knowing he wasn't.

'Never more serious,' said Alfie. Are you in, or not?'

I didn't know what to say. My mind was racing. My only hope was that the security was now much tighter round Silbury cuttings than it had been when the kid got killed. I swear Alfie could read my mind, because he reached into his bag and took out a pair of wire-cutters he'd pinched from his dad's toolbox.

I decided to play along with Alfie, till I could work out what to do. I told him I was in, then as soon as I could, I got Jamal and Leon on their own.

'Silbury cuttings!' said Jamal. 'No way! That's going too far.

Leon agreed and I was hugely relieved. Surely if all three of us said no, we could stop it? I mean, we didn't have votes or anything, but it was three against two, always assuming Dylan would even accept the dare. We should have known better.

We caught up with Alfie and Dylan before school on Friday. They were standing near the gate, deep in conversation. I felt a pang; it was like the good old days when we were all just best mates. Until we got close to them and we could see the look in their eyes.

They just refused to listen. Dylan said Alfie had set us all up to put him off, because then he could call him chicken. He was particularly disgusted with Jamal. So I did the unforgivable: I told them I'd tell their parents.

Alfie and Dylan rounded on me with identical looks of fury.

'If you do,' hissed Alfie, 'it'll be the end of you and me.'

I thought about being friends since before we were born.

'And.' He added, 'it won't even stop us. We'll just do it another time, when they've forgotten about it. They can't watch us for ever.'

I felt absolutely paralysed. The best we could do was to say that we wouldn't be there and that we thought they were both mad. We walked away into the school building and that was the moment I knew the Inliners had ended for ever.

But, of course, I did go to Silbury cuttings on Saturday afternoon and so did the others. I think we couldn't bear not to know what was going on. We squeezed through the gap in the wire fencing that Alfie had made with his father's cutters. Then we slid down the embankment and hid behind some bushes. We could see them, Dylan and Alfie, standing by the railway line like a couple of trainspotters. My mouth was dry: I could hear a train coming.

It streamed past and I had no idea what had happened. It was all noise and speed and confusion. I realised my eyes were shut. When I opened them, I could have cried with relief. Alfie and Dylan were both still standing there. But they seemed to be arguing. I caught the words 'not ready' before the wind whipped them away and I realised it wasn't all over. Dylan was still going to do it. I saw him step onto the line.

I think I must have gone a little mad then. I went charging down the embankment yelling. I don't even know what I was saying or what I intended to do. Wrestle them both to the ground and sit on them till they came to their senses? I was no Terminator.

There was another train coming. I grabbed Alfie, gibbering and crying like an idiot. The train was getting nearer. Dylan just stood there, white and frozen. He wasn't going to make it.

'Dylan!' I screamed, but he didn't seem to hear me. I didn't dare grab him. I still feel bad about that. I still have nightmares about it. Dylan standing on the line like a statue, me rooted to the spot, unable to move as the train got closer.

It was Alfie who moved. I felt him wrench himself away from my grasp and hurl himself towards Dylan. And then the train rushed by. I couldn't see them, couldn't hear anything but the screaming of wheels on rails. The slipstream from the speeding train knocked me over and I was out of it.

I came round hearing the others crashing down the embankment. Jamal and Leon helped me up and we saw the other two across the other side of the line. They were lying on the ground with their arms wrapped round one another, and there was a lot of blood.

Suddenly, there were shouts behind me. Policemen came down the embankment, talking urgently into their radios. They must have called the ambulance because that came flashing and nee-nawing along soon afterwards. It turned out someone had seen the hole in the chainlink fence and dialled 999. The police must have called the station too, because no more trains came by while the paramedics carried Dylan and Alfie away on stretchers.

The local papers tried to turn Alfie into a hero. He told me that was the worst part, having everyone praise him for saving Dylan's life, when his life wouldn't have been in any danger in the first place if it hadn't been for Alfie. He feels nothing but guilt about what happened. After all, he was okay, physically, just very shocked and bruised. But Dylan, well, his foot was so badly hurt, they had to amputate it.

He can't skate so well with his artificial one, but he still does it. We all still see each other. Alfie's parents didn't move away after all, and Dylan didn't pass his Grammar School exam, so we all ended up at the comprehensive. The funny thing is, although we're all still friendly, it's Alfie and Dylan who are best friends now.

Me and Alfie aren't as close as we used to be. I thought at first it was because he felt he owed Dylan one, but once he told me that it was more as if they had gone through a bad illness together and survived. 'It was a kind of madness,' he said.

We are definitely not a gang any more. Just a group of friends, who've known each other since Nursery. We wouldn't dare be anything else.

The Destructors
Graham Greene

It was on the eve of August Bank Holiday that the latest recruit became the leader of the Wormsley Common Gang. No one was surprised except Mike, but Mike at the age of nine was surprised by everything. 'If you don't shut your mouth,' somebody once said to him, 'you'll get a frog down it.' After that Mike kept his teeth tightly clamped except when the surprise was too great.

The new recruit had been with the gang since the beginning of the summer holidays, and there were possibilities about his brooding silence that all recognised. He never wasted a word even to tell his name until that was required of him by the rules. When he said 'Trevor' it was a statement of fact, not as it would have been with the others a statement of shame or defiance. Nor did anyone laugh except Mike, who finding himself without support and meeting the dark gaze of the newcomer opened his mouth and was quiet again. There was every reason why T., as he was afterwards referred to, should have been an object of mockery – there was his name (and they substituted the initial because otherwise they had no excuse not to laugh at it), the fact that his father, a former architect and present clerk, had 'come down in the world' and that his mother considered herself better than the neighbours. What but an odd quality of danger, of the unpredictable, established him in the gang without any ignoble ceremony of initiation?

The gang met every morning in an impromptu car-park, the site of the last bomb of the first blitz. The leader, who was known as Blackie, claimed to have heard it fall, and no one was precise enough in his dates to point out that he would have been one year old and fast asleep on the down platform of Wormsley Common Underground Station. On one side of the car-park leant the first occupied house, No. 3, of the shattered Northwood Terrace – literally leant, for it had suffered from the blast of the bomb and the side walls were supported on wooden struts. A smaller bomb and incendiaries had fallen beyond, so that the house stuck up like a jagged tooth and carried on the further wall relics of its neighbour, a dado, the remains of a fireplace. T., whose words were almost confined to voting 'Yes' or 'No' to the plan of operations proposed each day by Blackie, once startled the whole gang by saying broodingly, 'Wren built that house, father says.'

'Who's Wren?'

'The man who built St Paul's.'

'Who cares?' Blackie said. 'It's only Old Misery's.'

Old Misery – whose real name was Thomas – had once been a builder and decorator. He lived alone in the crippled house, doing for himself: once a week you could see him coming back across the common with bread and vegetables, and once as the boys played in the car-park he put his head over the smashed wall of his garden and looked at them.

'Been to the lav,' one of the boys said, for it was common knowledge that since the bombs fell something had gone wrong with the pipes of the house and Old Misery was too mean to spend money on the property. He could do the redecorating himself at cost price, but he had never learnt plumbing. The lav was a wooden shed at the bottom of the narrow garden with a star-shaped hole in the door: it had escaped the blast which had smashed the house next door and sucked out the window-frames of No. 3.

The next time the gang became aware of Mr Thomas was more surprising. Blackie, Mike and a thin yellow boy, who for some reason was called by his surname Summers, met him on the common coming back from the market. Mr Thomas stopped them. He said glumly, 'You belong to the lot that play in the car-park?'

Mike was about to answer when Blackie stopped him. As the leader he had responsibilities. 'Suppose we are?' he said ambiguously.

'I got some chocolates,' Mr Thomas said. 'Don't like 'em myself. Here you are. Not enough to go round, I don't suppose. There never is,' he added with sombre conviction. He handed over three packets of Smarties.

The gang was puzzled and perturbed by this action and tried to explain it away. 'Bet someone dropped them and he picked 'em up,' somebody suggested.

'Pinched 'em and then got in a bleeding funk,' another thought aloud.

'It's a bribe,' Summers said. 'He wants us to stop bouncing balls on his wall.'

'We'll show him we don't take bribes,' Blackie said, and they sacrificed the whole morning to the game of bouncing that only Mike was young enough to enjoy. There was no sign from Mr Thomas.

Next day T. astonished them all. He was late at the rendezvous, and the voting for that day's exploit took place without him. At Blackie's suggestion the gang was to disperse in pairs, take buses at random and see how many free rides could be snatched from unwary conductors (the operation was to be carried out in pairs to avoid cheating). They were drawing lots for their companions when T. arrived.

'Where you been, T.?' Blackie asked. 'You can't vote now. You know the rules.'

'I've been *there*,' T. said. He looked at the ground, as though he had thoughts to hide.

'Where?'

'At Old Misery's.' Mike's mouth opened and then hurriedly closed again with a click. He had remembered the frog.

'At Old Misery's?' Blackie said. There was nothing in the rules against it, but he had a sensation that T. was treading on dangerous ground. He asked hopefully, 'Did you break in?'

'No. I rang the bell.'

'And what did you say?'

'I said I wanted to see his house.'

'What did he do?'

'He showed it me.'

'Pinch anything?'

'No.'

'What did you do it for then?'

The gang had gathered round: it was as though an impromptu court were about to form and try some case of deviation. T. said, 'It's a beautiful house,' and still watching the ground, meeting no one's eyes, he licked his lips first one way, then the other.

'What do you mean, a beautiful house?' Blackie asked with scorn.

'It's got a staircase two hundred years old like a corkscrew. Nothing holds it up.'

'What do you mean, nothing holds it up. Does it float?'

'It's to do with opposite forces, Old Misery said.'

'What else?'

'There's panelling.'

'Like in the Blue Boar?'

'Two hundred years old.'

'Is Old Misery two hundred years old?'

Mike laughed suddenly and then was quiet again. The meeting was in a serious mood. For the first time since T. had strolled into the car-park on the first day of the holidays his position was in danger. It only needed a single use of his real name and the gang would be at his heels.

'What did you do it for?' Blackie asked. He was just, he had no jealousy, he was anxious to retain T. in the gang if he could. It was the word 'beautiful' that worried him – that belonged to a class world that you could still see parodied at the Wormsley Common Empire by a man wearing a top hat and a monocle, with a haw-haw accent. He was tempted to say, 'My dear Trevor, old chap,' and unleash his hell hounds. 'If you'd broken in,' he said sadly – that indeed would have been an exploit worthy of the gang.

'This was better,' T. said. 'I found out things.' He continued to stare at his feet, not meeting anybody's eye, as though he were absorbed in some dream he was unwilling – or ashamed – to share.

'What things?'

'Old Misery's going to be away all tomorrow and Bank Holiday.'

Blackie said with relief, 'You mean we could break in?'

'And pinch things?' somebody asked.

Blackie said, 'Nobody's going to pinch things. Breaking in – that's good enough, isn't it? We don't want any court stuff.'

'I don't want to pinch anything,' T. said. 'I've got a better idea.'

'What is it?'

T. raised eyes, as grey and disturbed as the drab August day. 'We'll pull it down,' he said. 'We'll destroy it.'

Blackie gave a single hoot of laughter and then, like Mike, fell quiet, daunted by the serious implacable gaze. 'What'd the police be doing all the time?' he said.

'They'd never know. We'd do it from inside. I've found a way in.' He said with a sort of intensity, 'We'd be like worms, don't you see, in an apple.' When we came out again there'd be nothing there, no staircase, no panels, nothing but just walls, and then we'd make the walls fall down – somehow.'

'We'd go to jug,' Blackie said.

'Who's to prove? and anyway we wouldn't have pinched anything.' He added without the smallest flicker of glee, 'There wouldn't be anything to pinch after we'd finished.'

'I've never heard of going to prison for breaking things,' Summers said.

'There wouldn't be time,' Blackie said. 'I've seen housebreakers at work.'

'There are twelve of us,' T. said. 'We'd organise.'

'None of us know how...'

'I know,' T. said. He looked across at Blackie. 'Have you got a better plan?'

'Today,' Mike said tactlessly, 'we're pinching free rides...'

'Free rides,' T. said. 'Kid stuff. You can stand down, Blackie, if you'd rather...'

'The gang's got to vote.'

'Put it up then.

Blackie said uneasily, 'It's proposed that tomorrow and Monday we destroy Old Misery's house.'

'Here, here,' said a fat boy called Joe.

'Who's in favour?'

T. said, 'It's carried.'

'How do we start?' Summers asked.

'He'll tell you,' Blackie said. It was the end of his leadership. He went away to the back of the car-park and began to kick a stone, dribbling it this way and that. There was only one old Morris in the park, for few cars were left there except lorries: without an attendant there was no safety. He took a flying kick at the car and scraped a little paint off the rear mudguard. Beyond, paying no more attention to him than to a stranger, the gang had gathered round T.; Blackie was dimly aware of the fickleness of favour. He thought of going home, of never returning, of letting them all discover the hollowness of T.'s leadership, but suppose after all what T. proposed was possible – nothing like it had ever been done before. The fame of the Wormsley common car-park gang would surely reach around London. There would be headlines in the papers. Even the grown-up gangs who ran the betting at the all-in wrestling and the barrow-boys would hear with respect of how Old Misery's house had been destroyed. Driven by the pure, simple and altruistic ambition of fame for the gang, Blackie came back to where T. stood in the shadow of Old Misery's wall.

T. was giving his orders with decision: it was as though this plan had been with him all his life, pondered through the seasons, now in his fifteenth year crystallised with the pain of puberty. 'You,' he said to Mike, 'bring some big nails, the biggest you can find, and a hammer. Anybody who can, better bring a hammer and a screwdriver. We'll need plenty of them. Chisels too. We can't have too many chisels. Can anybody bring a saw?'

'I can,' Mike said.

'Not a child's saw,' T. said. 'A real saw.'

Blackie realised he had raised his hand like any ordinary member of the gang.

'Right, you bring one, Blackie. But now there's a difficulty. We want a hacksaw.'

'What's a hacksaw?' someone asked.

'You can get 'em at Woolworth's,' Summers said.

The fat boy called Joe said gloomily, 'I knew it would end in a collection.'

'I'll get one myself,' T. said. 'I don't want your money. But I can't buy a sledge-hammer.'

Blackie said, 'They are working on No. 15. I know where they'll leave their stuff for Bank Holiday.

'Then that's all,' T. said. 'We meet here at nine sharp.'

'I've got to go to church,' Mike said.

'Come over the wall and whistle. We'll let you in.'

2

On Sunday morning all were punctual except Blackie, even Mike. Mike had a stroke of luck. His mother felt ill, his father was tired after Saturday night, and he was told to go to church alone with many warnings of what would happen if he strayed. Blackie had difficulty in smuggling out the saw, and then in finding the sledge-hammer at the back of No. 15. He approached the house from a lane at the rear of the garden, for fear of the policeman's beat along the main road. The tired evergreens kept off a stormy sun: another wet Bank Holiday was being prepared over the Atlantic, beginning in swirls of dust under the trees. Blackie climbed the wall into Misery's garden.

There was no sign of anybody anywhere. The lav stood like a tomb in a neglected graveyard. The curtains were drawn. The house slept. Blackie lumbered nearer with the saw and the sledge-hammer. Perhaps after all nobody had turned up: the plan had been a wild invention: they had woken wiser. But when he came close to the back door he could hear a confusion of sound hardly louder than a hive in swarm: a clickety-clack, a bang bang, a scraping, a creaking, a sudden painful crack. He thought: it's true, and whistled.

They opened the back door to him and he came in. He had at once the impression of organisation, very different from the old happy-go-lucky ways under his leadership. For a while he wandered up and down stairs looking for T. Nobody addressed him: he had a sense of great urgency, and already he could begin to see the plan. The interior of the house was being carefully demolished without touching the walls. Summers with hammer and chisel was ripping out the skirting-boards in the ground floor dining-room: he had already smashed the panels of the door. In the same room Joe was heaving up the parquet blocks, exposing the soft wood floorboards over the cellar. Coils of wire came out of the damaged skirting and Mike sat happily on the floor clipping the wires.

On the curved stairs two of the gang were working hard with an inadequate child's saw on the banisters – when they saw Blackie's big saw they signalled for it wordlessly. When he next saw them a quarter of the banisters had been dropped into the hall. He found T. at last in the bathroom – he sat moodily in the least cared-for room in the house, listening to the sounds coming up from below.

'You've really done it,' Blackie said with awe. 'What's going to happen?'

'We've only just begun,' T. said. He looked at the sledge-hammer and gave his instructions. 'You stay here and break the bath and the wash-basin. Don't bother about the pipes. They come later.'

Mike appeared at the door. 'I've finished the wires, T.,' he said.

'Good. You've just got to go wandering round now. The kitchen's in the basement. Smash all the china and glass and bottles you can lay hold of. Don't turn on the taps – we don't want a flood – yet. Then go into all the rooms and turn out the drawers. If they are locked get one of the others to break them open. Tear up any papers you find and smash all the ornaments. Better take a carving knife with you from the kitchen. The bedroom's opposite here. Open the pillows and tear up the sheets. That's enough for the moment. And you, Blackie, when you've finished in here crack the plaster in the passage up with your sledge hammer.'

'What are you going to do?' Blackie asked.

'I'm looking for something special,' T. said.

It was nearly lunch-time before Blackie had finished and went in search of T. Chaos had advanced. The kitchen was a shambles of broken glass and china. The dining-room was stripped of parquet, the skirting was up, the door had been taken off its hinges, and the destroyers had moved up a floor.

Streaks of light came in through the closed shutters where they worked with the seriousness of creators – and destruction after all is a form of creation. A kind of imagination had seen this house as it had now become.

Mike said, 'I've got to go home for dinner.'

'Who else?' T. asked, but all the others on one excuse or another had brought provisions with them.

They squatted in the ruins of the room and swapped unwanted sandwiches. Half an hour for lunch and they were at work again. By the time Mike returned they were on the top floor, and by six the superficial damage was completed. The doors were all off, all the skirtings raised, the furniture pillaged and ripped and smashed – no one could have slept in the house except on a bed of broken plaster. T. gave his orders – eight o'clock next morning, and to escape notice they climbed singly over the garden wall, into the car-park. Only Blackie and T. were left: the light had nearly gone, and when they touched a switch, nothing worked – Mike had done his job thoroughly.

'Did you find anything special?' Blackie asked.

T. nodded. 'Come over here,' he said, 'and look.' Out of both pockets he drew bundles of pound notes. 'Old Misery's savings,' he said. 'Mike ripped out the mattress, but he missed them.'

'What are you going to do? Share them?'

'We aren't thieves,' T. said. 'Nobody's going to steal anything from this house. I kept these for you and me – a celebration.'

He knelt down on the floor and counted them out – there were seventy in all. 'We'll burn them,' he said, 'one by one,' and taking it in turns, they held a note upwards and lit the top corner, so that the flame burnt slowly towards their fingers. The grey ash floated above them and fell on their heads like age. 'I'd like to see Old Misery's face when we are through,' T. said.

'You hate him a lot?' Blackie asked.

'Of course I don't hate him,' T. said. 'There'd be no fun if I hated him.' The last burning note illuminated his brooding face. 'All this hate and love,' he said, 'it's soft, it's hooey. There's only things, Blackie,' and he looked round the room crowded with the unfamiliar shadows of half things, broken things, former things. 'I'll race you home, Blackie,' he said.

3

Next morning the serious destruction started. Two were missing – Mike and another boy whose parents were off to Southend and Brighton in spite of the slow warm drops that had begun to fall and the rumble of thunder in the estuary like the first guns of the old blitz. 'We've got to hurry,' T. said.

Summers was restive. 'Haven't we done enough?' he asked. 'I've been given a **bob** for slot machines. This is like work.'

'We've hardly started,' T. said. 'Why, there's all the floors left, and the stairs. We haven't taken out a single window. You voted like the others. We are going to *destroy* this house. There won't be anything left when we've finished.'

They began again on the first floor picking up the top floorboards next the outer wall, leaving the joists exposed. Then they sawed through the joists and retreated into the hall,

---

bob a shilling, equivalent to 5p, but worth more when this story was written

as what was left of the floor heeled and sank. They had learnt with practice, and the second floor collapsed more easily. By the evening an odd exhilaration seized them as they looked down the great hollow of the house. They ran risks and made mistakes: when they thought of the windows it was too late to reach them. 'Cor,' Joe said, and dropped a penny down into the dry rubble-filled well. It cracked and span amongst the broken glass.

'Why did we start this?' Summers asked with astonishment; T. was already on the ground, digging at the rubble, clearing a space along the outer wall. 'Turn on the taps,' he said. 'It's too dark for anyone to see now, and in the morning it won't matter.' The water overtook them on the stairs and fell through the floorless rooms.

It was then they heard Mike's whistle at the back. 'Something's wrong,' Blackie said. They could hear his urgent breathing as they unlocked the door.

'The bogies?' Summers asked.

'Old Misery', Mike said. 'He's on his way,' he said with pride.

'But why?' T. said. 'He told me…' He protested with the fury of the child he had never been, 'It isn't fair.'

'He was down at Southend,' Mike said, 'and he was on the train coming back. Said it was too cold and wet.' He paused and gazed at the water. 'My, you've had a storm here. Is the roof leaking?'

'How long will he be?'

'Five minutes. I gave Ma the slip and ran.'

'We better clear,' Summers said. 'We've done enough, anyway.'

'Oh no, we haven't. Anybody could do this –' 'this' was the shattered hollow house with nothing left but the walls. Yet walls could be preserved. Façades were valuable. They could build inside again more beautifully than before. This could again be a home. He said angrily, 'We've got to finish. Don't move. Let me think.'

'There's no time,' a boy said.

'There's got to be a way,' T. said. 'We couldn't have got this far…'

'We've done a lot,' Blackie said.

'No. No, we haven't. Somebody watch the front.'

'We can't do any more.'

'He may come in at the back.'

'Watch the back too.' T. began to plead. 'Just give me a minute and I'll fix it. I swear I'll fix it.' But his authority had gone with his ambiguity. He was only one of the gang. 'Please,' he said.

'Please,' Summers mimicked him, and then suddenly struck home with the fatal name. 'Run along home, Trevor.'

T. stood with his back to the rubble like a boxer knocked groggy against the ropes. He had no words as his dream shook and slid. Then Blackie acted before the gang had time to laugh, pushing Summers backward. 'I'll watch the front, T.,' he said, and cautiously he opened the shutters of the hall. The grey wet common stretched ahead, and the lamps gleamed in the puddles. 'Someone's coming, T. No, it's not him. What's your plan, T.?'

'Tell Mike to go out to the lav and hide close beside it. When he hears me whistle he's got to count ten and start to shout.'

'Shout what?'

'Oh, "Help", anything.'

'You hear, Mike,' Blackie said. He was the leader again. He took a quick look between the shutters. 'He's coming, T.'

'Quick, Mike. The lav. Stay here, Blackie, all of you, till I yell.'

'Where are you going, T.?'

'Don't worry. I'll see to this. I said I would, didn't I?'

Old Misery came limping off the common. He had mud on his shoes and he stopped to scrape them on the pavement's edge. He didn't want to soil his house, which stood jagged and dark between the bomb-sites, saved so narrowly, as he believed, from destruction. Even the fan-light had been left unbroken by the bomb's blast. Somewhere somebody whistled. Old Misery looked sharply round. He didn't trust whistles. A child was shouting: it seemed to come from his own garden. Then a boy ran into the road from the car-park. 'Mr Thomas,' he called, 'Mr Thomas.'

'What is it?'

'I'm terribly sorry, Mr Thomas. One of us got taken short, and we thought you wouldn't mind, and now he can't get out.'

'What do you mean, boy?'

'He's got stuck in your lav.'

'He'd no business…Haven't I seen you before?'

'You showed me your house.'

'So I did. So I did. That doesn't give you the right to…'

'Do hurry, Mr Thomas. He'll suffocate.'

'Nonsense. He can't suffocate. Wait till I put my bag in.'

'I'll carry your bag.'

'Oh no, you don't. I carry my own.'

'This way, Mr Thomas.'

'I can't get in the garden that way. I've got to go through the house.'

'But you can get in the garden this way, Mr Thomas. We often do.'

'You often do?' He followed the boy with a scandalised fascination. 'When? What right…?'

'Do you see…? the wall's low.'

'I'm not going to climb walls into my own garden. It's absurd.'

'This is how we do it. One foot here, one foot there, and over.' The boy's face peered down, an arm shot out, and Mr Thomas found his bag taken and deposited on the other side of the wall.

'Give me back my bag,' Mr Thomas said. From the loo a boy yelled and yelled. 'I'll call the police.'

'Your bag's all right, Mr Thomas. Look. One foot there. On your right. Now just above. To your left.' Mr Thomas climbed over his own garden wall. 'Here's your bag, Mr Thomas.'

'I'll have the wall built up,' Mr Thomas said, 'I'll not have you boys coming over here, using my loo.' He stumbled on the path, but the boy caught his elbow and supported him. 'Thank you, thank you, my boy,' he murmured automatically. Somebody shouted again through the dark. 'I'm coming, I'm coming,' Mr Thomas called. He said to the boy beside him, 'I'm not unreasonable. Been a boy myself. As long as things are done regular. I don't mind you playing round the place Saturday mornings. Sometimes I like company. Only it's got to be regular. One of you asks leave and I say Yes. Sometimes I'll say No. Won't feel like it. And you come in at the front door and out at the back. No garden walls.'

'Do get him out, Mr Thomas.'

'He won't come to any harm in my loo,' Mr Thomas said, stumbling slowly down the garden. 'Oh, my rheumatics,' he said. 'Always get 'em on Bank Holiday. I've got to be careful. There's loose stones here. Give me your hand. Do you know what my horoscope said yesterday? "Abstain from any dealings in first half of week. Danger of serious crash." That might be on this path,' Mr Thomas said. 'They speak in parables and double meanings.' He paused at the door of the loo. 'What's the matter in there?' he called. There was no reply.

'Perhaps he's fainted,' the boy said.

'Not in my loo. Here, you, come out,' Mr Thomas said, and giving a great jerk at the door he nearly fell on his back when it swung easily open. A hand first supported him and then pushed him hard. His head hit the opposite wall and he sat heavily down.

His bag hit his feet. A hand whipped the key out of the lock and the door slammed. 'Let me out,' he called, and heard the key turn in the lock. 'A serious crash,' he thought, and felt dithery and confused and old.

A voice spoke to him softly through the star-shaped hole in the door. 'Don't worry, Mr Thomas,' it said, 'we won't hurt you, not if you stay quiet.'

Mr Thomas put his head between his hands and pondered. He had noticed that there was only one lorry in the car-park, and he felt certain that the driver would not come for it before the morning. Nobody could hear him from the road in front, and the lane at the back was seldom used. Anyone who passed there would be hurrying home and would not pause for what they would certainly take to be drunken cries. And if he did call 'Help', who, on a lonely Bank Holiday evening, would have the courage to investigate? Mr Thomas sat on the loo and pondered with the wisdom of age.

After a while it seemed to him that there were sounds in the silence – they were faint and came from the direction of his house. He stood up and peered through the ventilation hole – between the cracks in one of the shutters he saw a light, not the light of a lamp, but the wavering light that a candle might give. Then he thought he heard the sound of hammering and scraping and chipping. He thought of burglars – perhaps they had employed the boy as a scout, but why should burglars engage in what sounded more and more like a stealthy form of carpentry? Mr Thomas let out an experimental yell, but nobody answered. The noise could not even have reached his enemies.

4

Mike had gone home to bed, but the rest stayed. The question of leadership no longer concerned the gang. With nails, chisels, screwdrivers, anything that was sharp and penetrating, they moved around the inner walls, worrying at the mortar between the bricks. They started too high, and it was Blackie who hit on the damp course and realised the work could be halved if they weakened the joints immediately above. It was a long, tiring, unamusing job, but at last it was finished. The gutted house stood there balanced on a few inches of mortar between the damp course and the bricks.

There remained the most dangerous task of all, out in the open at the edge of the bomb-site. Summers was sent to watch the road for passers-by, and Mr Thomas, sitting on the loo, heard clearly now the sound of sawing. It no longer came from the house, and that a little reassured him. He felt less concerned. Perhaps the other noises too had no significance.

A voice spoke to him through the hole. 'Mr Thomas.'

'Let me out,' Mr Thomas said sternly.

'Here's a blanket,' the voice said, and a long grey sausage was worked through the hole and fell in swathes over Mr Thomas's head.

'There's nothing personal,' the voice said. 'We want you to be comfortable tonight.'

'Tonight,' Mr Thomas repeated incredulously.

'Catch,' the voice said. 'Penny buns – we've buttered them, and sausage-rolls. We don't want you to starve, Mr Thomas.'

Mr Thomas pleaded desperately. 'A joke's a joke, boy. Let me out and I won't say a thing. I've got rheumatics. I got to sleep comfortable.'

'You wouldn't be comfortable, not in your house, you wouldn't. Not now.'

'What do you mean, boy?' But the footsteps receded. There was only the silence of night: no sound of sawing. Mr Thomas tried one more yell, but he was daunted and rebuked by the silence — a long way off an owl hooted and. made away again on its muffled flight through the soundless world.

At seven next morning the driver came to fetch his lorry. He climbed into the seat and tried to start the engine. He was vaguely aware of a voice shouting, but it didn't concern him. At last the engine responded and he backed the lorry until it touched the great wooden shore that supported Mr Thomas's house. That way he could drive right out and down the street without reversing. The lorry moved forward, was momentarily checked as though something were pulling it from behind, and then went on to the sound of a long rumbling crash. The driver was astonished to see bricks bouncing ahead of him, while stones hit the roof of his cab. He put on his brakes. When he climbed out the whole landscape had suddenly altered. There was no house beside the car-park, only a hill of rubble. He went round and examined the back of his lorry for damage, and found a rope tied there that was still twisted at the other end round part of a wooden strut.

The driver again became aware of somebody shouting. It came from the wooden erection which was the nearest thing to a house in that desolation of broken brick. The driver climbed the smashed wall and unlocked the door. Mr Thomas came out of the loo. He was wearing a grey blanket to which flakes of pastry adhered. He gave a sobbing cry. 'My house,' he said. 'Where's my house?'

'Search me,' the driver said. His eye lit on the remains of a bath and what had once been a dresser and he began to laugh. There wasn't anything left anywhere.

'How dare you laugh,' Mr Thomas said. 'It was my house. My house.'

'I'm sorry,' the driver said, making heroic efforts, but when he remembered the sudden check of his lorry, the crash of bricks falling, he became convulsed again. One moment the house had stood there with such dignity between the bomb-sites like a man in a top hat, and then, bang, crash, there wasn't anything left – not anything. He said, 'I'm sorry. I can't help it, Mr Thomas. There's nothing personal, but you got to admit it's funny.'

Porkies
Robert Swindells

Piggo Wilson was an eleven-plus failure. We *all* were at Lapage Street Secondary Modern School, or *Ecole Rue laPage* as we jokily called it. Eleven-plus was this exam kids used to take in junior school. It was crucial, because it more or less decided your whole future. Pass eleven-plus and you qualified for a grammar school education, which meant you went to a posh school where the kids wore uniforms and got homework and learned French and Latin and went on trips to Paris. At Grammar School you left when you were sixteen to start a career, or you could stay on till you were eighteen and go to university. *Fail* eleven-plus and you were shoved into a Secondary Modern School where you wore whatever happened to be lying around at home and learned reading, writing and woodwork. You couldn't get any qualifications and you left on your fifteenth birthday and got a job in a shop or factory. Not a *career:* a job.

One of the rottenest things about being an eleven-plus failure was that you knew you'd let your mum and dad down. *Everybody*'s parents hoped their kid would pass and go to the posh school. Some offered bribes: *pass your eleven-plus son, and we'll buy you a brand new bike*. Others threatened: *fail your eleven-plus son, and we'll drag yer down the canal and drown yer.* But grammar school places were limited and there were always more fails than passes.

It wasn't nice, knowing you were a failure. Took some getting used to, especially if your best friend at junior school had passed. You'd go and call for him Saturday morning same as before, only now his mum would answer the door and say, 'Ho, hai'm hafraid William hasn't taime to come out and play: he's got his Latin homework to do.' *William*. It was Billy before the exam. You'd call round a few more times, then it'd dawn on you that you wouldn't be playing with *William* any more. Grammar School boy, see: can't be seen mixing with the peasants.

Most kids took it badly one way or another, but it seemed to bear down particularly heavily on Piggo. The rest of us compensated by jeering at the posh kids, whanging stones at them or beating them up, but that didn't satisfy Piggo. What he started doing was telling these really humungous lies about himself. He'd stroll into the playground Monday mornings and say something like, 'Went riding Saturday afternoon with my grandad, bagged a wildcat.' He'd say it with a straight face as well, even though everybody *knew* he'd never been anywhere near a horse in his life and wildcats lived in Scotland. In fact if you pointed this out he'd say, 'Yes, that's where we rode to, Scotland.' Or we'd be listening to Dick Barton on the wireless and he'd say, 'My *dad*'s a special agent too, y'know: works with Barton now and then.' If you pointed out that Dick Barton was a fictional character he'd wink and tell you that was Barton's cover story. He couldn't help it, old Piggo: he needed to feel he was special to make up for everybody else seeing him as a failure.

Anyway that's how things were, and by and by it got to be 1953. There was something special about 1953, even at Lapage Street Secondary Modern School, because of two momentous events which took place that year. One was the coronation of the young Queen Elizabeth at Westminster Abbey. 'My cousin'll be there,' claimed Piggo, 'she's a lady-in-waiting.'' She's a lady in *Woolworth's*,' said somebody: a correction Piggo chose to ignore.

The other momentous event was the conquest of Mount Everest. For decades, expeditions from all over the world had battled to reach the summit of the world's highest peak, and many climbers had hurtled to their deaths down its icy face. Finally, in 1953, a British expedition succeeded in putting two men on the summit. They planted the Union Jack and filmed it snapping in a freezing wind. The pictures went round the world and the people of Britain surfed on a great wave of national pride: a wave made all the more powerful because it was coronation year.

As coronation day approached, and while the Everest expedition was still only in the foothills of the Himalayas, our teachers decided that Lapage Street Secondary Modern School would stage a patriotic pageant to mark the Queen's accession to the throne, and to celebrate the dawn of a New Elizabethan Age with poetry, song and spectacle. A programme was worked out. Rehearsals began. An invitation was posted to the Lord Mayor who promised to put in an appearance on the day, should his busy schedule permit.

We failures were excited, not by all these preparations but by the prospect of the day's holiday we were to get on coronation day itself, and the souvenir mug crammed with toffees every child in the land was to receive. I say *all*, but it would be more accurate to say *all but one* of us was excited. While the rest of us laboured to memorise a very long poem about Queen Elizabeth the First and hoarded our pennies to buy tiny replicas of the coronation coach, Piggo Wilson sank into a long sulk because he couldn't get anybody to believe his latest story, which was that Mount Everest had actually been conquered years ago in a solo effort by his uncle.

He'd tried it on Ma Lulu first. Her real name was Miss Lewis. She was the only woman teacher in our all-boys' school and she took us for Divinity, which is called RE now. On the day the news broke that Sir John Hunt's expedition had planted the Union Jack on the roof of the world, she was talking to us about the courage and endurance of Sherpa Tensing and Edmund

Hillary, the two men who'd actually reached the summit, when Piggo's hand went up.

'Yes, Wilson?' We didn't use first names at Lapage.

'Please Miss, they weren't the first.'

Ma Lulu frowned. *'Who* weren't? What're you blathering about, boy?'

'Hillary and Sherpa whatsit, Miss. They weren't the first, my uncle was.'

'Your *uncle?*' She glared at Piggo. We were all sniggering. We daren't laugh out loud because Ma Lulu had two rulers bound together with wire which she liked to whack knuckles with. Rattling, she called it.

'Are you asking us to believe that an uncle of yours *climbed Mount Everest,* Wilson?'

'Yes, Miss.'

'Rubbish! Who *told* you this, Wilson? Or are you making it up as you go along, I expect that's it, isn't it?'

'No Miss, my dad told me. My uncle was his brother, Miss.' Sniggers round the room.

'What's his name, this uncle?'

'Wilson Miss, same as me, only he's dead now.'

'His *first* name, laddie: what was his first name?'

'Maurice Miss: Maurice Wilson.'

'Well *I've* never heard of a mountaineer called Maurice Wilson,' She appealed to the class. 'Has anybody else?'

We mumbled, shook our heads. 'No,' snapped Ma Lulu, 'of course you haven't, because there's no such person.' She glared at Piggo. 'If this uncle of yours had conquered Mount Everest, Wilson, *everybody* would know his name: it would have become a household word as Hillary has, and Tensing.'

'But Miss, he didn't get back so it couldn't be proved. Some people say he never reached the top, Miss.'

'Wilson,' said Ma Lulu patiently, 'two weeks ago I set this class an essay on the parable of the Good Samaritan. You wrote that you'd been to Jericho for your holidays and stayed at the actual inn.' She regarded him narrowly. 'That wasn't quite true, was it?'

'No Miss,' mumbled Piggo.

'Where did you *actually* spend those holidays, laddie?'

'Skegness Miss.'

'Skegness.' She arched her brow. 'Does Jesus mention Skegness at all in that parable, Wilson?'

'No Miss.'

'No Miss He does not, and why? Because Jesus never visited Skegness, and your uncle never visited Everest.' She sighed. 'I don't know what's the matter with you, Wilson: not only do you insult *me* by interrupting my lesson with your nonsense, you insult those brave men who risked their lives to plant the Union Jack on the roof of the world. Open your jotter.'

Piggo opened his jotter. 'Write this: *I have never been to Jericho, and my claim that my uncle climbed Mount Everest is another wicked lie, of which I am deeply ashamed.*' Piggo wrote laboriously, the tip of his tongue poking out. When he'd finished Ma Lulu said, 'You will write that out a hundred times in your very best handwriting and bring it to me in the morning.'

We all had a good laugh at Piggo's expense, but an amazing thing happened next morning. Instead of presenting his hundred lines, Piggo brought his dad. He didn't look like a special agent, but nobody'd expected him to. We watched the two of them across the yard, but we had to wait till morning break to find out what it was all about. Turned out Piggo's late uncle *had* made a solo attempt on Everest back in the thirties and had been found a year later 7,000 feet below the summit, frozen to death. The climbers who found him claimed they also found the Union Jack he'd taken with him, which seemed to prove he hadn't reached the summit, but the story in the Wilson family was that Maurice had taken *two* flags, left one on the peak and died on the way down. The climbers had found his spare. The fact that nobody outside the family believed this didn't worry them at all.

Ma Lulu probably didn't believe that part either, but she was as gobsmacked as the rest of us to learn that Piggo's tale was even *partly* true. She apologised handsomely, cancelled his punishment *and* used our next Divinity lesson to tell us the story of Maurice Wilson's brave if foolhardy attempt to conquer the world's highest peak all by himself. We were a bit wary of Piggo after that, but taunted him slyly about his family's version of the outcome. He stuck to his guns, insisting that his uncle had beaten Tensing and Hillary by more than twenty years.

Our pageant came and went. The Lord Mayor didn't. He had another engagement but his deputy attended, wearing his modest chain of office. Some parents came too. Piggo's mum was one of them, which is how we found out she wasn't a Siamese twin as her son had insisted. On coronation day school was closed. There were very few TVs then, so most people listened to bits of the ceremony on the wireless. Most *adults* I mean. We kids had better things to do, like setting the golf-course on fire as an easy way of uncovering the lost balls we sold to players at a shilling each.

For us, the best bit of that momentous year came a few weeks later. The Headmaster announced in assembly that a local cinema was to show films in colour of the coronation ceremony, including the Queen's procession through London in her golden coach, *and* of the conquest of Everest, compiled from footage shot by expedition members, including the final assault on the peak and views from the summit. Pupils from schools across the city would go with their teachers to watch history being made in this stupendous double bill. There'd be no charge, and our school was included.

We could hardly wait, and Piggo was even more impatient than the rest of us. 'Now you'll see,' he crowed, 'it'll show the peak just before those losers Tensing and Hillary stepped on to it and my uncle's flag'll be there, flapping in the wind.' We smiled pityingly and shook our heads, but he seemed so confident that as the day approached, our smug certainty wavered a bit.

It was at the Ritz, right in the middle of the city. A fleet of coaches had been laid on to carry the hundreds of kids from schools all over the district. Ours didn't arrive first. We piled off and joined a queue that curved right round the building. The class in front of us was from one of the grammar schools so we spat wads of bubblegum, aiming at their hair and the backs of their smart blazers. Red-faced teachers darted about, yanking kids out of the queue and shaking them, hissing through bared teeth, *'D'you think Her Majesty spat bubblegum all over Westminster Abbey: did Sherpa Tensing spag a wad from the summit to see how far it would go, eh?'* It made the time pass till they started letting us in.

They ran the coronation first. It was quite a spectacle, the scarlet and gold of the uniforms and regalia sumptuous in the grey streets, but it didn't half go on. We got bored and began taunting Piggo. 'Which one's your cousin then, Wilson: you know, the lady-in-waiting?'

'Ssssh!' went some teacher, but it was dark: he couldn't see who was talking. 'Come on Wilson,' we urged, 'point her out.' Piggo made a show of craning forward to peer at the faces in the procession. There were hundreds. After a bit he pointed to an open carriage that was being pulled by four horses. 'There!' he cried, 'that's her, in that cart.' Just then the camera zoomed in, revealing that the woman was black. We shouted with laughter, and Piggo muttered something about having relatives in the colonies. As the camera lingered on her face, the commentator told us the woman was the Queen of Tonga.

The film dragged on. A great aunt of mine, who had a bit of money and owned the only TV in our family, had had people round on coronation day. Those early TVs had seven-inch screens, the picture was black and white, or rather black and a weird *bluish* colour, the image so fuzzy you had to have the curtains drawn if you wanted to see anything. Coverage had lasted all day, and my great aunt's guests had sat with their eyes glued to it from start to finish. *Get a life* I suppose we'd say nowadays, but it was the novelty: none of those people had seen a TV before. Anyway, I was thankful not to have been there.

The Everest film was a great deal more interesting to kids like us. Much of it had been shot with hand-held cameras on treacherous slopes in howling gales so you got quite a lot of camera-shake, but the photographers had captured some breathtaking scenery, and it was interesting to see mountaineers strung out across the snowfield roped together, stumping doggedly upward with ice-clotted beards. Another interesting thing was the mounds of paraphernalia lying around their camps: oxygen cylinders, nylon tents, electrically-heated snowsuits, radio transmitters and filming equipment, not to mention what looked like *tons* of grub and a posse of Sherpas to hump everything. Brought home to us how pathetically underequipped Piggo's uncle had been with his three loaves and two tins of oatmeal, his silken flag. Or had it been *two* silken flags?

Underequipped anyway.

We sat there gawping, absorbed but waiting for the climax: that first glimpse of the summit which would silence poor Piggo once and for all, and he was impatient too, confident we'd see his uncle's flag and be forced to eat our words. It was a longish film, but presently the highest camp was left behind and we were seeing shaky footage of Tensing: 'Tiger,' the press would soon christen him, inching upward against the brilliant snow, and of Hillary, filmed by the Sherpa. We were getting occasional glimpses of the peak too, over somebody's labouring shoulder, but it was too distant for detail. There was what looked like a wisp of white smoke against the blue, as though Everest were a volcano, but it was the wind blowing snow off the summit.

Presently a note of excitement entered the narrator's voice and we sat forward, straining our eyes. The lead climber had only a few feet to go. The camera, aimed at his back, yawed wildly, shooting a blur of rock, sky, snow. Any second now it'd steady, focusing on the very, very top of the world. We held our breath, avid to witness this moment of history whether it included a silken flag or not.

The moment came and there was no flag. No flag. *There* was the tip of Everest, sharp and clear against a deep blue sky and it was pristine. Unflagged and, for a moment longer, unconquered. A murmur began in thirty throats and swelled, the sound of derision. 'Wilson you *moron,*' railed someone, 'where is it, eh: where *is* your uncle's silken flipping flag?'

Piggo sat gutted. Crushed dumb. We watched as he shrank, shoulders hunched, seeming almost to *dissolve* into the scarlet plush of the seat. Fiercely we exulted at his discomfiture, his humiliation, knowing there'd be no more bragging, no more porkies from this particular piggo. The film ended and we filed out, nudging him, tripping him up, sniggering in his ear.

We were feeling so chipper that when we got outside we looked around for some posh kids to kick, but they'd gone. This small disappointment couldn't dampen our spirits however. We knew that what had happened inside that cinema: the final, irrevocable sinking of Piggo Wilson was what we'd remember of 1953. We piled on to our coach, which pulled out and nosed through the teatime traffic, bound for *Ecole Rue laPage*. When we came to a busy roundabout the driver had to give way. In the middle of the roundabout was a huge equestrian statue; the horse rearing up, the man wearing a crown and brandishing a sword. Piggo, who'd been sitting very small and very quiet, pointed to the statue of Alfred the Great and said, 'See the feller on the horse there: he was my grandad's right-hand man in the Great War.'

Billy the Kid
William Golding

On the first day, Lily, my nurse, took me to school. We went hand-in-hand through the churchyard, down the Town Hall steps, and along the south side of the High Street. The school was at the bottom of an alley; two rooms, one downstairs and one upstairs, a staircase, a place for hanging coats, and a lavatory. 'Miss' kept the school – handsome, good-tempered Miss, whom I liked so much. Miss used the lower room for prayers and singing and drill and meetings, and the upper one for all the rest. Lily hung my coat up, took me upstairs, and deposited me among a score or so of children who ranged in age from five to eleven. The boys were neatly dressed, and the girls overdressed if anything. Miss taught in the old-fashioned way, catering for all ages at once.

I was difficult.

No one had suggested, before this time, that anything mattered outside myself. I was used to being adored, for I was an attractive child. Indeed, my mother would declare that I had 'eyes like cornflowers and hair like a field of ripe corn.' I had known no one outside my own family – nothing but walks with Lily or my parents and long holidays by a Cornish sea. I had read much for my age but saw no point in figures. I had a passion for words in themselves, and collected them like stamps or birds' eggs.

I had also a clear picture of what school was to bring me. It was to bring me fights. I lacked opposition, and yearned to be victorious.

It did not occur to me that school might have discipline or that numbers might be necessary. While, therefore, I was supposed to be writing out my tables, or even dividing four oranges between two poor boys, I was more likely to be scrawling a list of words, butt (barrel), butter, butt (see goat). While I was supposed to be learning my Collect, I was likely to be chanting inside my head a list of delightful words which I had picked up – deebriss and skirmishar, creskent and sweeside. On this first day, when Miss taxed me with my apparent inactivity, I smiled and said nothing until she went away.

I had quickly narrowed my interest in school to the quarter of an hour between eleven and fifteen minutes past. This was Break, when our society at last lived up to my expectations. While Miss sat at her desk and drank tea, we spent the Break playing and fighting in the space between the desks and the door. The noise rose slowly in shrillness and intensity, so that I could soon assess the exact note at which Miss would ring a handbell and send us back to our books. If we were dull and listless, Break might be extended by as much as ten minutes; so there was a constant conflict in my mind – a desire to be rowdy, and a leader in rowdiness, together with the knowledge that success would send us back to our desks.

The games were numerous and varied with our sex. The girls played with dolls or at weddings. Most of the time they played Postman's Knock among themselves – played it seriously, like a kind of innocent **apprenticeship**.

Tap! Tap!

'Who's there?'

'A letter for Mary.'

We boys ignored them with a contempt of inexpressible depth. We did not kiss each other, not we. We played tag or fought in knots and clusters.

---

apprenticeship the process of learning a profession

Fighting proved to be just as delightful as I had thought. I was chunky and **zestful** and enjoyed hurting people. I exulted in victory, in the complete **subjugation** of my **adversary**, and thought that they should enjoy it too – or at least be glad to suffer for my sake. For this reason, I was puzzled when the supply of opponents diminished. Soon I had to corner victims before I could get a fight at all.

There were whisperings in corners and on the stairs. There were meetings. There were conversations which ceased when I came near. Suddenly in Break, when I tried to fight, the opposition fled with screams of hysterical laughter, then combined in democratic strength and hurled itself on my back. As for the little girls, they no longer played Postman's Knock, but danced on the skirts of the scrum, and screamed encouragement to the just majority.

That Break ended early. When we were back at our desks, I found my rubber was gone, and no one would lend me another. But I needed a rubber, so I chewed up a piece of paper and used that. Miss detected my fault and cried out in mixed horror and amusement. Now the **stigma** of dirt was added to the others.

At the end of the morning I was left disconsolate in my desk. The other boys and girls **clamoured out** purposefully. I wandered after them, puzzled at a changing world. But they had not gone far. They were grouped on the cobbles of the alley, outside the door. The boys stood warily in a semicircle, their satchels swinging loose. The girls were ranged behind them, ready to send their men into the firing line. The girls were excited and giggling, but the boys were pale and grim.

---

zestful enthusiastic
subjugation defeat
adversary opponent
stigma disgrace
clamoured out went out, making a lot of noise

'Go on!' shouted the girls. 'Go on!'

The boys took cautious steps forward.

Now I saw what was to happen – felt shame, and the bitterness of all my seven beings. Humiliation gave me strength. A rolled-up exercise book became an epic sword. I went mad. With what felt like a roar, but must really have been a pig-squeal, I leapt at the nearest boy and hit him squarely on the nose. Then I was round the semi-circle, hewing and thumping. The screams of the little girls went needle sharp. A second or two later, they and the boys were broken and running up the alley, piling through the narrow entry, erupting into the street.

I stood alone on the cobbles and a wave of passionate sorrow engulfed me. Indignation and affront, shame and frustration took command of my muscles and my lungs. My voice rose in a sustained howl, for all the world as though I had been the loser. I began to zigzag up the alley, head back, my voice serenading a vast sorrow in the sky. My feet found their way along the High Street, and my sorrow went before me like a brass band. Past the Antique Shoppe, the International Stores, Barclay's Bank; past the tobacconist's and the *Green Dragon,* with head back, and grief as shrill and steady as a siren...

I suspected that my reservoirs were not sufficient for the waters of **lamentation**, suspected that my voice would disappear, and that I was incapable of a half-mile's sustained emotion. I began to run, therefore, so that my sorrow would last. When suspicion turned to certainty, I cut my crying to a whimper and settled to the business of getting it home. Past the *Aylesbury Arms,* across the London Road, through Oxford Street by the Wesleyan Chapel, turn left for the last climb in the Green – and there my feeling inflated like a balloon, so that I did the last twenty yards

---

lamentation grief

as tragically as I could have wished, swimming through an ocean of sorrow, all quite genuine – swung on the front-door knob, stumbled in, staggered to my mother…

'Why, Billy! Whatever's the matter?'

… balloon burst, floods, tempests, hurricanes, rage and anguish – a monstrous yell…

'THEY DON'T LIKE ME!'

My mother administered consolation and the hesitant suggestion that perhaps some of the transaction had been my fault. But I was beyond the reach of such **footling** ideas. She comforted, my father and Lily hovered, until at last I was quiet enough to eat. My mother put on her enormous hat and went out with an expression of grim purpose. When she came back, she said she thought everything would be all right. I continued to eat and sniff and hiccup. I brooded righteously on what was going to happen to my schoolfellows now that my mother had taken a hand. They were, I thought, probably being sent to bed without anything to eat, and it would serve them right and teach them to like me and not be cruel. After lunch, I enjoyed myself darkly inventing possible punishments for them – lovely punishments.

Miss called later and had a long talk with my mother in the drawing-room. As she left, I stuck my field of ripe corn round the dining-room door again and saw them.

'Bring him along a quarter-of-an-hour late,' said Miss. 'That's all I shall need.'

Next day at school everyone was seated and you could have stuck a fork into the air of noiseless excitement. Wherever I looked there were faces that smiled shyly at me. I inspected them for signs of damage but no one seemed to have suffered any

footling trivial

crippling torment. I reached for a rubber, and a girl in pink and plaits leaned over.

'Borrow mine.'

A boy offered me a handkerchief. Another passed me a note with 'wil you jine my ggang' written on it. I was in. We began to say our tables and I only had to pause for breath before giving an answer to six sevens for a gale of whispers to suggest sums varying from thirty-nine to forty-five. Dear Miss had done her work well, and today I should enjoy hearing her fifteen minutes' sermon on brotherly love. Indeed, school seemed likely to come to a full stop from sheer excess of charity; so Miss, smiling remotely, said we would have an extra long Break. My heart leapt, because I thought that now we could get on with some really fierce, friendly fighting, with even a bloody nose. But Miss produced a train set. When the other boys got down to fixing rails, the girls, inexpressibly moved by the sermon, seized me **in posse**. I never stood a chance against those excited arms, those tough, silken chests, those bird-whistling mouths, that mass of satin and **serge** and wool and pigtails and ribbons. Before I knew where I was, I found myself, my cornflower eyes popping out of my head, playing Postman's Knock.

The first girl to go outside set the pattern.

'A parcel for Billy Golding!'

In and out I went like a weaver's shuttle, pecked, pushed, hugged, mouthed and mauled, in and out from fair to dark to red, from Eunice who had had fever and a **crop**, to big Martha who could sit on her hair.

I kissed the lot.

---

in posse as a group
serge woollen fabric
crop a short hairstyle

This was, I suppose, my first lesson; and I cannot think it was successful. For I did not know about the sermon then. I merely felt that the boys and girls who tried to do democratic justice on me had been shown to be wrong. I was, and now they knew it, a thoroughly likeable character. I was unique and precious after all; and I still wondered what punishments their parents had found for them which had forced them to realise the truth.

I still refused to do my lessons, confronting Miss with an **impenetrable** placidity. I still enjoyed fighting if I was given the chance. I still had no suspicion that Billy was anything but perfect. At the end of term, when I went down to Cornwall, I sat in a crowded carriage with my prize book open on my knees for six hours, so that passengers could read the inscription. I am reading it now:

Billy Golding

1919

Prize for

General Improvement

---

impenetrable impossible to break through

The Cats
Robert Westall

Today, there was a cat in the house.

There has been no cat even in the grounds for thirty years, since we bought it. My dogs have seen to that. I am a dog person.

I came in from the garden, stripping off my gardening gloves, my eyes full of sunlight, thinking about nothing in particular. I went upstairs to get changed for tea. And there it was sitting at the head of the stairs, perfectly at home, looking down on me as if *I* were the intruder.

I hate cats. But I had to admit it was a prime specimen. A blotched tabby, with great thick gouts of pure black running down its coat. Almost, in the sunlight on the stair, a black cat, with stripes of golden guard hairs like networks of stars. Big. Fat. Silently purring; so hard it was rocking slightly with pleasure, the way cats do. As if it had got something it had waited for a long time. Certainly the purring was not for me; its eyes, staring into mine, were as cold as green ice. As cold as mine, I suppose. It looked at me as if it were my equal – as if it were my superior. Its claws were extending and retracting in time with its purring.

I waved my gloves in its face, shooed at it.

It did not move. It held its place. You may say it could not get past me, down the stairs... It did not even want to get past me. It wanted to keep me out of my own house.

I grew uneasy, as I stood there, on the sixth step down. I noticed again how big it was; how big the claws, extending and contracting. On the top step, it was nearly level with my face. It looked ... a nasty beggar to tackle. Animals should know the rules. My dogs have always known the rules. This cat didn't. And when animals don't know the rules...

I backed down a few steps. Called to my dogs, knowing they wouldn't be far behind me, coming in from the garden, yawning and stretching.

They did not come; they did not answer, useless brutes. Nervous, I turned back quickly to face the cat, frightened it might spring.

It was gone from the stair-head. It was not in the upstairs corridor. And all the doors were shut, except the one to my husband's study. I went in, in a bit of a temper. My husband used to be very fond of cats, when he was young. I had a feeling he might have encouraged this one...

But he was asleep, in the swivel-chair at his desk, a, big book on the Adriatic open on his knees. He was having his fallow time, as he calls it. He had finished this year's play for the West End. At the end of August, we were going off to the Adriatic, for this year's travel book. He spends his fallow time reading and dozing in the sun. When you're nearly seventy, I suppose it's permissible. He does work hard when he *is* working...

His face looked, somehow, different. A little ... transparent. You watch them, when they get to that age. But he was breathing very softly, normally. So I just put it down to the late afternoon sun that was flooding the room with light. In any case, he awakened then; stretched and smiled. To himself, not at me. He hadn't even realised I was there.

'Nice dream?' I asked.

He closed his eyes again, instantly. The wrinkles round his closed mouth moved, resorting themselves into a new expression. Then he opened his eyes and looked at me, and said 'Can't remember it. But, yes, nice...'

Liar, I thought. Whatever your dream was, I wouldn't have been welcome in it. I was cross, so I said, 'There was a damned cat on the stairs. Hasn't been in here, has it?'

'I've seen no cat. What colour was it?' Once he's got his defensive wall up, there's no getting past it.

'Big tabby thing. Fat and cocky. Faced up to me, on my own staircase. Didn't give a damn.'

'You should've set your dogs on it!'

'Damned dogs were nowhere to be seen.' He was laughing at me, inside himself. I can always tell.

Then he said, 'The cat sounds a bit like old Mirabelle.' He spoke as if Mirabelle were still around, not dead for nearly forty years. Then I knew he was really sticking his knife into me.

So I went and had a shower.

Showers usually set me up; but not this one. I took the late Mirabelle in with me, and brought her out again. Mirabelle was the cat he had when I first met him. When he was plain Harry Tremblett, failed poet and pub crawler, not Sir Harold Tremblett, playwright, travel writer and critic. Living in a three-room basement in King's Cross, with rows of dirty milk bottles at the door, and rows of empty wine bottles by the area dustbins. God knew how he kept himself in booze; God knew how he could bear to live in that slum of unmade bed and dirty plates with the cold tap dripping on them, and an old wind-up gramophone piled with scratched 78's of Bunk Johnson and Bessie Smith. And the queen of that slum was Mirabelle, with her knowledgeable eyes that had seen everything and told nothing.

I don't know how I ever brought myself to make love on that bed, with that cat watching, that first time. Afterwards, the cat came sliding over, fussing at him, licking his sweating face, trying to force herself between us, so that he accused her of being jealous, and laughed with delight.

She lasted a long time, did Mirabelle – longer than the unmade bed or the dirty plates or the rows of empties; longer even than all his revolting friends: the well-heeled amateur communists, the duffle-coated anarchists, and the ex-girlfriends who thought they could absorb me into their **complaisant** ranks.

Mirabelle was the last thing to go. It was after my father got him that temporary lectureship at Leeds, the first step he made up the ladder. I'd arranged everything: the university flat where pets were forbidden, even the friends who would take Mirabelle off our hands.

Then, the day before we left, Mirabelle got ill. Suddenly she was uncontrollably messing all over the flat. It's lucky we were packed by that time.

I told him, 'You can't expect my friends to have her now – messing all over the place. She'll have to *go*, Harry.'

He gaped at me. 'Go *where*?'

'Be put to sleep. She's over ten years old...'

'But the vet could make her better...'

'And how much would *that* cost? Treatment and drugs and kennel bills. You've hardly got the train fare to Leeds...'

'Lend me the money...'

'No. I've lent you *enough*. I have to earn it, the hard way. I'm not wasting it on a damned cat.'

He sat down and took her on his knee, a little gingerly. He glared at me and said, 'I'm not going to Leeds. You can stuff your bloody Leeds and your stinking little bourgeois lectureship. I'm staying here with Mirabelle, and I'm going to make her well, and we're going to live here and be *happy*.'

---

complaisant accepting

'You've given up the lease,' I said. 'The new people are moving in tomorrow, God help them.'

'I'm not going...'

'Suit yourself. I'll tell my father you're resigning, that you don't want the flat up there. And you won't be seeing any more of me. Blow this chance, and we're *finished.*'

He put his head down. I didn't realise he was crying till the drops of water began hitting Mirabelle's tangled fur. God, I can't stand men who cry; it just disgusts me. So I threw down a couple of pound notes on to the old washed-out mattress and said, 'That's to pay for the vet – to put her down. And if you're not at the station by the time the train goes, it's bye-bye.'

Then Mirabelle finished herself off. She gave a low, mournful cry, and messed on the trousers of his only half-decent suit.

I didn't stay to be argued with. I picked up my suitcase and left. I will never forget the look the cat gave me, as I walked out the door. It was as if she *knew.*

Harry was at the station on time.

Alone.

Back in the shower I told myself I was being stupid, and towelled myself dry too vigorously, so I broke out sweating again.

By the time I'd dressed, I'd convinced myself the cat on the stairs was nothing like Mirabelle. The world was full of large, fat, arrogant blotched tabbies. The world was also full of slightly dotty sixty-three-year-old women, so I'd better pull myself together before I joined them.

The end of August is like a great tide going out. The world is suddenly too full of trees and the trees are too full of leaves and the leaves fade from green to dark grey like an old photograph left too long in the glaring sun. And even the quality of the sunlight fails – not the quantity, but the quality. It is almost as if the eyes have had too much sunlight, and can't take it in any more, so that there is a sudden darkness in the midst of the sunlight. And the heat is a dead heat; the dead heat of a kiln just turned off because the final temperature has been reached. And all your friends are far away, and all the village organisations are asleep. Even the vicar is away, and the Sunday service is taken by some **uncouth** and nervous stranger from the nearest town. And the Final Test drones down to an endless hopeless draw. I listen to the sleepy commentary, and I imagine the players, lost in the dark sunlight, moving slower and slower, and the commentator's eyelids drooping. Someone, before the First World War, wrote a novel in which the Germans invaded on August Bank Holiday, and won because nobody on our side could bother to mobilise. That writer knew August.

I am a doer. I have a horror of nothing to do. I have been a doer all my life. If I cannot do, I begin to cease to be. I grasped at tiny things, like straws. I was glad that Mrs Temple our housekeeper had gone to Ibiza with her husband; so that at least I had the cooking and dusting. I swept up the first **errant** autumn leaves when there were not enough to make a trug-full. I cut down plants long before their time. I made sudden despairing telephone calls to town, to people who I had lost touch with for years, only to find they were away too.

Harry does not seem to mind. He reads; he sleeps in the sun. He does not sprawl disgustingly in his sleep like some elderly men. He curls up gracefully, like a cat. He smiles in his sleep, like a cat. Like a cat, it is impossible to tell if he is *really* asleep when I come into the room, or just pretending. Even awake,

---

uncouth unrefined
errant straying

he is oddly far away, further away than he has ever been. It makes me nervous. I try to coax him into doing things. But he knows they are needless. He will do them when autumn comes, after we are back from the Adriatic. Or we will get a man to do them...

I don't press him. We have always had this bargain. He has written his play for the year. Soon, he will begin gathering stuff for his travel book. Fair's fair.

So why does it make me so afraid?

I have seen another cat. A quite different cat. A long-haired white cat, playing in and out of the shrubbery, under the shadow of the dark rhododendron leaves, like a moth fluttering at a lamplit window after dark, coming and going.

I shouted at it when I came round the corner of the house. Waved my arms to scare it. It paused, looked at me with dark empty eyes from a head like a beautiful skull. Then went on flitting, in and out.

Harry was asleep on the lounger, under the French windows which were open to cool the house. I gave him a too-rough poke, because I was seized with the awful irrational fear that he might be dead. He came awake, smiling again, as if he'd had yet another pleasant dream.

'There was another cat,' I said, crossly. 'Didn't you see it?'

'Where?' he said.

And he looked straight at the shrubbery. When he could've looked anywhere.

'What colour was it?'

'White,' I said, flatly. 'A white long-hair. Playing in that shrubbery – where you were just looking.'

'I can't see any cat.' Was he laughing at me again?

'It's gone now,' I said shortly.

'Funny – it's always you who sees them. It isn't as if you're a lover of them. A white long-hair you say? Sounds like Imogen's cat, Suki...'

Imogen.

Imogen Smallbridge. I first heard her name over the telephone, when Derek Pither phoned me from Rome. He said he wanted a quiet little word with me. Derek was famous for his quiet little words; few could have been as **devastating** as the one I got.

Harry had gone off the rails. In Rome. Right in the middle of a lecturing tour for the British Council that I had worked heavens hard to get him. He had missed giving his talk in Florence, and the one in Venice was due that day and there was no sign of Harry. And Derek had a jolly good idea where Harry and Imogen Smallbridge had gone. A boat she had hired for the summer, tied up in Malta.

I flew straight out, cursing my own stupidity. It was the first time in five years I'd let Harry off the reins.

We reached Valetta harbour that evening in one of those ridiculous horse-drawn things. Upset as I was, I had to pause as I got down from that ridiculous smelly old open carriage.

Valetta harbour is grand theatre. The huge stone quays, the nooks and crannies of water, leading out of sight; the houses peering one over the other, like people in the **gods** at a theatre; the distant domes. It was a very fine sunset: all the western half of the harbour was already slipping into blue shadow, but the eastern half glowed as if freshly cast in gold. The air was like a soothing warm bath on my bare arms. I was bitterly entranced – what an evening to be happy, if the world had been different.

---

devastating shocking
gods the balcony, the top tier of seats

The water of the harbour, filthy as it was, looked fresh and pale blue. There was an aircraft carrier at anchor; we still had carriers in those days. A three-funnelled troopship full of troops returning from Egypt was just sliding in to anchor alongside. Rows of silent sailors watched from the carrier; rows of soldiers in khaki drill stared back silently from the troopship. I was caught up in that magic that can accompany the worst misery.

Then the troopship anchor rattled down, and a single voice of coarse jeering called to the carrier from the troopship.

'Get yer knees brown!'

And in a moment, there was a barrage of insults from both ships, and the magic was broken forever, and Derek Pither, little fat balding Derek with his bad breath, who I could never stand, but whom I clung to now, pointed down to where a white boat lay against the quay, already overcome by blue shadow.

We went down an endless succession of worn sandy treacherous steps, and crept aboard like thieves. I remember the gap between the boat and the quay: oily water full of small oranges and the bloated body of a dog, with a swollen belly that the hair was starting to fray off. The gangway I crossed sagged as I stepped on it, and I nearly missed the handrail and fell into the water, and didn't really care.

All I remember about the boat was that it was big and white, and didn't seem in very good repair. Patches of white paint had flaked off, and the handrails were rusty. From the upraised ventilator of a skylight a scratchy gramophone record played. Bessie Smith's coarse voice yelling. I knew I had found him. Even before I saw the long-haired white cat, sitting at the top of the **companionway**, almost like a schoolboy keeping watch for his friends.

---

companionway the steps leading down from the deck to the cabin

The cat looked at me, and I looked at the cat. It was bold, bolder than any dog would dare to be. Stared me out, its only sign of anxiety a front paw raised in the air as if about to strike me. Then its eyes faltered from left to right; it licked its lips and swallowed twice. I swung at it wildly with my bag, and with a spit it had wriggled through a gap of open door and run down inside.

I heard Harry's voice say languidly, 'What's the matter, Suki? What's upset you?'

And then I stormed down out of the sunlight and air into the dark cabin.

The smell of booze; booze and bodies. Not dead bodies; living blatant bodies. The smell of frying and French cigarettes.

They were sitting on a padded couch with lockers underneath it. The padding of the leather was scuffed. Harry's white shirt, which two weeks ago I'd washed and ironed, was filthy and open at the neck. There were spots on his lightweight trousers, and he didn't seem to have bothered to comb his hair. None of which surprised me, any more than the row of empties stacked at the top of the companionway had.

What surprised me was Imogen Smallbridge. I had been expecting a tart; I would've welcomed a tart. I could have quickly dismissed a tart from my memories. Imogen Smallbridge was not a tart. She looked every inch the lady. Tall, slim, in clean white slacks and an open-necked shirt of white and green bands. Neat leather sandals on long neat clean feet. An enviably long neck, dark hair pulled tightly back in a bun. About thirty-five, and the knuckles of her long hands already enlarged with arthritis. Her spectacles gave her an intellectual look, but her cheekbones were beautiful, and her eyes the saddest I have ever seen. You can see why I would've welcomed a tart.

'Who is it?' asked Harry in a cheerful voice. 'Do we know you?' I was in silhouette against the light of the companionway;

he hadn't recognised me yet. So I had a long moment to savour their togetherness, the relaxedness of their bodies sitting side by side, the hands coiled together loosely because of the sweaty heat. It was the way he said 'we' that hurt so much. Oh, yes, I remember them in their cosy paradise. And the cat at their feet, glaring at me as if it would like to kill me, paw uplifted to strike, ears back.

I won't go into all that passed between us. Suffice to say that in the end I gave Harry the same old choice. He still wasn't established then. His job was better, but still the gift of my father. The man who was publishing Harry's first travel book was a friend of my father; so was the magazine editor who gave Harry poetry books to review.

Harry came to the airport on time. I watched him say goodbye to Imogen Smallbridge at the gate to the airport. I never asked what he said to her.

Two weeks later, she got the engine of her boat going, and sailed out into one of those savage little storms they get off Malta. Neither she nor her hired boat were ever seen again.

I suppose the white cat went with her.

I don't think he cared for any of them, after Imogen Smallbridge. I even think he went out of his way to choose girls who would not be hurt when they lost him. As far as I ever found out, none of them vanished in tragic circumstances. They smiled and forgot him. After all, it was the Swinging Sixties. He didn't try to hide them. I was always aware when a thing started. A strange smell on his clothes as I picked them up for the laundry basket. And the cat hairs on his trousers, of course, that I could stroke up into thick whorls with my hand. So I could tell what colour of cat it was this time. I didn't try to break any more of his 'things' up. I thought he was getting a taste for histrionic scenes, and in the Swinging Sixties, histrionic scenes were getting more and more ridiculous. It was a bad time to be a possessive wife. It was a good time to be a girl with a pet cat.

I never thought of leaving him. There was too much to do. He was having his great successes. *Hard Morning* at the Royal Court. *Sunderland Boy* at the Roundhouse, and then in the West End. As the Sixties drew on, and Wesker faded out of sight, and Pinter stuck at a certain level, and Osborne went embarrassing, Harry turned a little more popular in his views. Tough plays for the soft-hearted. **Provocative** plays you could safely take your mother-in-law to. *Darkling Thrush* at the Duke of York's. *Ambuscade* at the Prince of Wales. Even that damned musical that ran and ran, *Midsummer Morning*. Then he was the Royal choice: Sir Harold Tremblett, up there with Sir Terence Rattigan, Sir Harold Hobson and Sir John Gielgud. A knight of the theatre, welcome on any TV discussion panel, putting the view of the intelligent decent common man.

I think he started to ease up in his private life, by the beginning of the seventies. After all he was over fifty, and success is *so* exhausting. But he made up for it with the cats, as he gave up going to bed with their owners. Any walk with him became a nightmare. He would spend hours crouched on his heels at some set of area railings, trying to coax the staring cat behind to come and be fondled. He kept a pocket full of those new cat-biscuits, to make sure they would follow us home through the hot summer streets.

I don't think he ever thought of leaving me, either. He needed a tyrant to rebel against, a fascist dictatorship at home to make symbolic protests against, because it was too much bother to go and howl at the protest crowds in Trafalgar Square any more. So cosy to have your own dictator handy.

Provocative deliberately causing a strong response

I must stop writing. There is a large ginger cat sitting staring at me, from the top of the garden wall. It has been there nearly half an hour, just staring. There are so many cats getting into the garden now. Every time I garden, I find their paw-prints in the wet mud on the paths after a shower; their scrabblings amidst my flowers; their hollowed-out resting places among my lavender bushes. The dogs do not deter them. It often seems to me the dogs are scared of them.

Why are they coming? I am afraid.

This afternoon I got home and called out to Harry as I came in the front door.

There was no reply. Frankly, it terrified me. He is such a creature of habit, usually. He writes in the mornings, until one. In the afternoon, he reads, or lounges, or goes for a little walk, no doubt to find cats to talk to. In the evening, we have people in, or go out ourselves, or watch television.

He could not be out for a walk today. It had been nice, earlier in the afternoon, but a hot wind had got up, and storm-clouds had been gathering ominously. Anyone could tell there was going to be a storm, and Harry is as sharp about weather changes as a cat, And like cats, he hates wind and rain. Where was he? I ran upstairs to his study, thinking he might be asleep and might not have heard my calling.

He wasn't there. He wasn't in any of the upstairs rooms. I heard a door bang downstairs. Bang, bang. Then a tinkle of glass. The French windows...

The French windows were banging in the wind. There was glass on the living-room carpet. And outside, in his lounger, Harry lay, asleep, the rising wind ruffling his silver hair, the first drops of rain from the storm falling on him. Around him sat four cats. And there was a grey cat lying on his chest. They were all staring at his face. Then they seemed to sense me, and turned to stare at me.

Have you ever been stared at by five cats together? With hate in their eyes? For a moment, I couldn't move. I could only watch the movements of the huge thin straggly grey cat that lay upon Harry's chest. Its paws were in constant movement, kneading at the wool of the grey jumper he wore, the claws going in and out, pounding at him just where his heart was.

I might have stood forever, caught in the web of those five sets of eyes, if the French windows hadn't banged again, breaking another pane of glass.

I ran at them, shouting. Screaming my head off, actually.

The French windows seemed to have slammed shut. I wrestled desperately with the handle, and then they were open again, and I fell through, tripping over the step and almost going full-length across Harry and the lounger.

He opened his eyes sleepily, bewildered. 'Helen!'

'Wha—' I pushed myself up by my hands, and stared around. There wasn't a cat in sight. Just a scatter of yellow autumn leaves, blowing across the patio, lodging round the legs of Harry's lounger. And the increasing **shilling**-sized spots of rain.

I got him indoors by main force, as the storm started in earnest. He seemed very sluggish, dazed. I took him into the kitchen, and made us both a strong cup of tea.

The tea seemed to revive him, though he still looked very pale and drawn. He said, almost to himself, 'I've been asleep. I've been a long way away.'

'You *have* been asleep. With that great cat on your chest...' I was too frightened and relieved to nag him.

---

shilling a coin about 2.5 cm in diameter

'Which great cat?' He seemed genuinely surprised for once – not having me on.

'A great big grey scraggy thing. Long hair. Thin as a rake...'

'I don't like grey cats,' he said, and shuddered. 'I don't like thin cats. I like fat cats.' He really did seem bewildered.

'It doesn't remind you of any lady's cat in particular, then?' I was getting back the courage to be spiteful.

He shook his head, thoughtfully. 'I never knew anyone with a thin grey cat. I don't like them.' He shuddered again.

'You've got yourself chilled,' I said. 'What made you go out with a storm brewing up?'

'It was sunny when I went out there. After lunch. I must have dozed off.'

'You must have been asleep over an hour. What were you thinking of?'

'I must've been very tired. I didn't sleep well last night.'

Suddenly his face changed, and he said, 'I am glad to see you.'

'And I'm glad to see you. I leave you too much on your own...'

He smiled at me. 'Perhaps you do.'

For some reason, I held his hand, and he let me.

'I won't leave you alone so much in future,' I said.

'Good. I think I'll have a bath, to warm myself up.' He got up stiffly. Suddenly, for the first time, I thought of him as old; someone to be looked after.

I lit the fire in the lounge, though I didn't put on the central heating. It didn't seem cold enough for that, though with the storm it had got colder. We had our supper by the fire, and were cosy.

Just before I switched on the television he said to me, 'We haven't been very nice to each other, have we, Helen?'

'It's not been bad, these last ten years. We've stopped hurting each other...'

'Yes, we've stopped hurting each other ... like an old cat and an old dog who've got too old for the game.'

'Would you rather we'd gone on hurting each other?'

He smiled oddly. 'It was fun ... in the old days.'

'It wasn't fun for me,' I said shortly. And switched on the television. I've regretted turning on that damned set ever since. I think he wanted to talk to me, for the first time, really, in years. But I was tired, and still shaken. I didn't want to be shaken any more, that night. As you get older, you can't take it any more. And yet, as I turned on the set, I thought wistfully of the nights we stayed up to have a row all night, when we were young. We meant that much to each other, then. We'd make up, make love, with the first of the dawn streaking through the bedroom curtains, and lie snuggled tight and warm till lunchtime and someone frantically ringing the doorbell.

Two days later, Harry went up to London to see his publisher and spend the night at his house. He disliked the long journey to London, and liked a night to recover before coming back. I smiled to myself as I made my hot-water bottle (for the weather had really turned cold, as it sometimes does at the end of August, and electric blankets were not in the beds yet).

I had let Harry off the hook again. He was on his own in London. He might be doing anything... Just like old times. In a perverse way, I almost liked the thought. It made me feel younger, somehow. Especially as I knew my fancy was rubbish. Harry was too old, and Paul Deane much too thorough a host and raconteur. Still, some imp of fancy made me ring Paul Deane's house, playing some foolish charade of being the wronged and suspicious wife.

Of course, Paul Deane himself answered, and said he and Harry were in the library, having a last brandy and putting the world to bed. Did I want a word with him? Harry came on, a little baffled at such wifely concern, but mellow with brandy, and, I think, a little touched and sentimental. We said quite a fond goodnight.

I started up the stairs.

And the blotched tabby was there again. Staring down at me, with that infinite knowing air of superiority.

I was not frightened. I had just heard Harry's voice, warm and relaxed, two hundred miles away and quite safe. I just went berserk, that a cat should dare to invade my new-found glow of happiness.

'The dogs will settle you,' I said to it. 'Just you wait and see.' I went back down to the kitchen, where the dogs were already curled up sleepily in their beds.

They wagged their tails feebly, but refused to move. They seemed … apologetic. It wasn't typical. An invitation to come upstairs with me, last thing at night, is usually greeted with great enthusiasm. I'm afraid I lost my temper and grabbed their collars and began to haul them out to the hall by main strength. They fought me all the way, squirming and collapsing in a heap, whining and licking their lips. Cringing.

I got them as far as the foot of the stairs, dragging them across the shiny parquet. Golden Labradors are a fair weight, especially when they are starting to get a bit old and fat, but I did it, one hand through each collar. I realise now that I couldn't have been in a normal mood, even at that point.

At the foot of the stairs, they collapsed completely, just squirming trembling heaps of slack bone and muscle. Keening soft and low in their throats. I despaired, and let go of their collars. Immediately they fled back to the kitchen.

And still I was not afraid. The dogs' leads hang on the hall stand. One of them is a thing I've never liked: half a leash and half a whip – a kind of plaited **sjambok** thing from South Africa, that could be used to beat a dog half to death. I had never dreamt of using it on poor Rory and Bruce; I would not use it on any animal, even as a leash. I hated it.

But now I picked it up. That thing on the stairs was not an animal; it was a fiend that was persecuting me; I would destroy it...

I ran up the stairs. It saw the whip; a quick glance, then its arrogant eyes were back on my face, rejecting, hating, taunting. I was crazed by its arrogance. I raised the whip, and brought it down with all my strength.

It missed, and hit the stair carpet with a force that stung my hand.

I could not understand how I could have missed. I could not understand how the beast had not moved or even flinched but continued to glare up at me, half-crouched, ears back, mouth open in a silent snarl. I struck again and again, each time harder than the last.

And each time I missed. Hit the top step instead, with a sound like a hollow drum.

The world was insane; the world was twisting under my mind into unbelievable shapes. I could *not* go on missing at this range. The cat could not still be there, snarling silent defiance.

And then I watched my next blow carefully, with what sanity I could still muster.

I was not missing. The whip passed straight through the cat and hit the carpet beneath it.

The next second, the blotched tabby cat was no longer there.

---

sjambok a whip made of rhinoceros hide

Not in the upper hall, with all its doors closed. Not in the lower hall, which was bare and well lit. And certainly not in the kitchen with the dogs.

Not in the house at all. I sat in the lounge a long time, trembling and drinking whisky, over the revived remains of the log fire.

I finally went up to bed as dawn broke, and some kind of order returned to the world. I went up to bed without hope of sleeping. I think I hoped I might lie on my bed fully-dressed and doze for a few hours, before facing another day.

But something made me stop at the closed door of Harry's study. I was a long time opening that door.

When I did, the blotched tabby was sitting on Harry's desk in the window. I could not see any detail of it, because it was hunched on his pile of foolscap paper, against the light. But from the way it rocked, I knew that it was purring.

The house is full of cats now. They flick at the corners of my eye, and then when I look, they are gone – under a chair, behind a couch. But I know there is no point in searching for them. They are all ghosts. And yet, in the corner of my eye, I seem to see them quite clearly; a sort of detailed blur. It is often the long-haired white cat. Imogen's cat. Its fur is sleeked close to its skin, as if it had just emerged from water. There is a ginger cat with a white chest. There is a black cat that is no more than two green eyes, glaring out of the shadow beneath a chair.

I ignore them, as I ignore the cats in the garden. I think the cats in the garden are real, for they leave paw prints. I do not mind them; they only sit and stare at the house, as if waiting for something.

They are waiting for Harry. He is ill. The doctor does not know what is the matter. They have done tests, and can find nothing wrong. The doctor talks of overwork, of Harry needing to rest. But he has been resting for three weeks now. He never needed so much rest any other August. And the more he rests, the more he sleeps, the wearier he is. He hardly bothers to read, now. He picks up a book **listlessly**, and then I come back in ten minutes, and he is dozing over it. I think the cats are draining his life away; and he is letting them.

When he is awake, he is very affectionate. He kisses my hand. He says I have looked after him very well. He says I have done my best, according to my lights. He forgives me for everything I have ever done to him...

I would rather that he hated me. Then there would be some hope. Then there would be something to hold him to this world.

Tonight, he said, 'I'm sorry, Helen. I went too far away. I can't get back.'

Before I could ask him what he meant, he had fallen asleep again.

My one consolation is that the cats mean him no harm. I know that in their own way they love him.

It is me they hate.

I have put the dogs into kennels. Left here, they did nothing but cower in their beds. They would not eat, and their toilet training was breaking down. I rang the kennels this morning. They are quite happy there, and recovering rapidly.

I have just come down from Harry's study. I was going to his bedroom, to see if he wanted anything, when something made me open the study door. He was sitting in his desk chair, with his back turned to the desk and the window, the way he always sits when he is stuck in his writing, and thinking. He had his head up; he looked better than he had done for weeks. He was

---

listlessly without energy

actually *dressed*, in a baggy old pair of trousers and sloppy old sweater I thought I'd thrown out years ago. I could not see him well against the light, but I saw his cheek curve out in silhouette as he smiled at me, that old lazy smile.

'You're better!' I said, amazed and glad.

'Yes,' he said, 'I'm all right now. It was a worrying time, but it's over. I'm fine, now.'

I began to weep, from sheer relief.

He said kindly, affectionately, 'Don't cry now. I'm sorry you've been so worried. I've been a burden to you. I've made your life wretched...'

'That doesn't matter. It doesn't matter at all. We've got to look to the future. There's so much still to do.'

'Yes,' he said, and smiled again. 'There's still so much to do.' He sounded glad.

I took a step towards him, a step into the room. It gave me a clearer look at him, because the swivel-chair is big and enclosing, with high back and arms, like half an egg on a swivel.

I saw there was a cat sitting in his lap.

A blotched tabby. Not snarling at me now, but rocking, purring, triumphant.

And I watched his hand go down to caress her. I expected to see his hand pass straight through her.

It didn't. It rested gently on her back. I saw her fur bend beneath it. They were together, as they had been so long ago, in that wretched flat in King's Cross.

'Goodbye, Helen,' he said. 'Goodbye and thanks and sorry. I am me, and you are you. Who am I to cast the first stone?'

And then the chair was empty.

I did not go to the bedroom. I knew what I should find. The house is empty. No more ghosts. How I wish there could be ghosts, now. The real cats are still sitting in the garden, front paws together, and tails wrapped round. They are so still, they might be statues. They look ceremonial, like mourners. They are paying their respects to Harry.

I must ring the doctor; or the ambulance or the police.

I only wish I could move from this chair.

The Brazilian Cat
Arthur Conan Doyle

It is hard luck on a young fellow to have expensive tastes, great expectations, aristocratic connections, but no actual money in his pocket and no profession by which he may earn any. The fact was that my father, a good, sanguine, easy-going man, had such confidence in the wealth and benevolence of his bachelor elder brother, Lord Southerton, that he took it for granted that I, his only son, would never be called upon to earn a living for myself. He imagined that if there were not a vacancy for me on the great Southerton Estates, at least there would be found some post in that diplomatic service which still remains the special preserve of our privileged classes. He died too early to realise how false his calculations had been. Neither my uncle nor the state took the slightest notice of me or showed any interest in my career. An occasional brace of pheasants, or basket of hares, was all that ever reached me to remind me that I was heir to Otwell House and one of the richest estates in the country. In the meantime, I found myself a bachelor and man about town, living in a suite of apartments in Grosvenor Mansions, with no occupation save that of pigeon-shooting and polo-playing at Hurlingham. Month by month, I realised that it was more and more difficult to get the brokers to renew my bills or to cash any further post-obits upon an unentailed property. Ruin lay right across my path, and every day I saw it clearer, nearer and more absolutely unavoidable.

What made me feel my own poverty the more was that, apart from the great wealth of Lord Southerton, all my other relations were fairly well-to-do. The nearest of these was Everard King, my father's nephew and my own first cousin, who had spent an adventurous life in Brazil and had now returned to this country to settle down on his fortune. We never knew how he made his money, but he appeared to have plenty of it, for he bought the estate of Greylands, near Clipton-on-the-Marsh, in Suffolk. For the first year of his residence in England he took no more notice of me than my miserly uncle; but at last one summer morning, to my very great relief and joy, I received a letter asking me to come down that very day and spend a short visit at Greylands Court. I was expecting a rather long visit to Bankruptcy Court at the time, and this interruption seemed almost providential. If I could only get on terms with this unknown relative of mine, I might pull through yet. For the family credit, he could not let me go entirely to the wall. I ordered my valet to pack my valise, and I set off the same evening for Clipton-on-the-Marsh.

After changing at Ipswich, a little local train deposited me at a small, deserted station lying amidst a rolling grassy country, with a sluggish and winding river curving in and out amidst the valleys, between high, silted banks, which showed that we were within reach of the tide. No carriage was awaiting me (I found afterwards that my telegram had been delayed), so I hired a dogcart at the local inn. The driver, an excellent fellow, was full of my relative's praises, and I learned from him that Mr Everard King was already a name to conjure with in that part of the country. He had entertained the schoolchildren, he had thrown his grounds open to visitors, he had subscribed to charities – in short, his benevolence had been so universal that my driver could only account for it on the supposition that he had parliamentary ambitions.

My attention was drawn away from my driver's **panegyric** by the appearance of a very beautiful bird which settled on a

---

panegyric a speech in praise of someone or something

telegraph-post beside the road. At first I thought that it was a jay, but it was larger, with a brighter plumage. The driver accounted for its presence at once by saying that it belonged to the very man whom we were about to visit. It seems that the acclimatisation of foreign creatures was one of his hobbies, and that he had brought with him from Brazil a number of birds and beasts which he was endeavouring to rear in England. When once we had passed the gates of Greylands Park we had ample evidence of this taste of his. Some small spotted deer, a curious wild pig known, I believe, as a peccary, a gorgeously feathered oriole, some sort of armadillo and a singular lumbering in-toed beast like a very fat badger were among the creatures which I observed as we drove along the winding avenue.

Mr Everard King, my unknown cousin, was standing in person upon the steps of his house, for he had seen us in the distance and guessed that it was I. His appearance was very homely and benevolent, short and stout, forty-five years old, perhaps, with a round, good-humoured face, burned brown with the tropical sun and shot with a thousand wrinkles. He wore white linen clothes, in true planter style, with a cigar between his lips and a large panama hat upon the back of his head. It was such a figure as one associates with a verandahed bungalow, and it looked curiously out of place in front of this broad, stone English mansion, with its solid wings and its Palladio pillars before the doorway.

'My dear!' he cried, glancing over his shoulder; 'my dear, here is our guest! Welcome, welcome to Greylands! I am delighted to make your acquaintance, Cousin Marshall, and I take it as a great compliment that you should honour this sleepy little country place with your presence.'

Nothing could be more hearty than his manner, and he set me at my ease in an instant. But it needed all his cordiality to atone for the frigidity and even rudeness of his wife, a tall, haggard woman, who came forward at his summons. She was, I believe, of Brazilian extraction, though she spoke excellent English, and I excused her manners on the score of her ignorance of our customs. She did not attempt to conceal, however, either then or afterwards, that I was no very welcome visitor at Greylands Court. Her actual words were, as a rule, courteous, but she was the possessor of a pair of particularly expressive dark eyes, and I read in them very clearly from the first that she heartily wished me back in London once more.

However, my debts were too pressing and my designs upon my wealthy relative were too vital for me to allow them to be upset by the ill-temper of his wife, so I disregarded her coldness and reciprocated the extreme cordiality of his welcome. No pains had been spared by him to make me comfortable. My room was a charming one. He implored me to tell him anything which could add to my happiness, It was on the tip of my tongue to inform him that a blank cheque would materially help towards that end, but I felt that it might be premature in the present state of our acquaintance. The dinner was excellent, and as we sat together afterwards over his Havanas and coffee, which later he told me was specially prepared upon his own plantation, it seemed to me that all my driver's **eulogies** were justified, and that I had never met a more large-hearted and hospitable man.

But, in spite of his cheery good nature, he was a man with a strong will and a fiery temper of his own. Of this I had an example upon the following morning. The curious aversion which Mrs Everard King had conceived towards me was so strong that her manner at breakfast was almost offensive. But her meaning became unmistakable when her husband had quitted the room.

---

eulogies praise

'The best train in the day is at twelve fifteen,' said she.

'But I was not thinking of going today,' I answered, frankly – perhaps even defiantly, for I was determined not to be driven out by this woman.

'Oh, if it rests with you –' said she, and stopped with a most insolent expression in her eyes.

'I am sure,' I answered, 'that Mr Everard King would tell me if I were outstaying my welcome.'

'What's this? What's this?' said a voice, and there he was in the room. He had overheard my last words, and a glance at our faces had told him the rest. In an instant his chubby, cheery face set into an expression of absolute ferocity.

'Might I trouble you to walk outside, Marshall,' said he? (I may mention that my own name is Marshall King.)

He closed the door behind me, and then, for an instant, I heard him talking in a low voice of concentrated passion to his wife. This gross breach of hospitality had evidently hit upon his tenderest point. I am no eavesdropper, so I walked out on to the lawn. Presently I heard a hurried step behind me, and there was the lady, her face pale with excitement and her eyes red with tears.

'My husband has asked me to apologise to you, Mr Marshall King,' said she, standing with downcast eyes before me.

'Please do not say another word, Mrs King.'

Her dark eyes suddenly blazed out at me.

'You fool!' she hissed, with frantic vehemence, and turning on her heel swept back to the house.

The insult was so outrageous, so insufferable, that I could only stand staring after her in bewilderment. I was still there when my host joined me. He was his cheery, chubby self once more.

'I hope that my wife has apologised for her foolish remarks,' said he.

'Oh, yes – yes, certainly!'

He put his hand through my arm and walked with me up and down the lawn.

'You must not take it seriously,' said he. 'It would grieve me inexpressibly if you curtailed your visit by one hour. The fact is – there is no reason why there should be any concealment between relatives – that my poor dear wife is incredibly jealous. She hates that anyone – male or female – should for an instant come between us. Her ideal is a desert island and an eternal tete-a-tete. That gives you the clue to her actions, which are, I confess, upon this particular point, not very far removed from mania. Tell me that you will think no more of it.'

'No, no; certainly not.'

'Then light this cigar and come round with me and see my little menagerie.'

The whole afternoon was occupied by this inspection, which included all the birds, beasts and even reptiles which he had imported. Some were free, some in cages, a few actually in the house. He spoke with enthusiasm of his successes and his failures, his births and his deaths, and he would cry out in his delight, like a schoolboy, when, as we walked, some gaudy bird would flutter up from the grass, or some curious beast slink into the cover. Finally he led me down a corridor which extended from one wing of the house. At the end of this there was a heavy door with a sliding shutter in it, and beside it there projected from the wall an iron handle attached to a wheel and a drum. A line of stout bars extended across the passage.

'I am about to show you the jewel of my collection,' said he. 'There is only one other specimen in Europe, now that the Rotterdam cub is dead. It is a Brazilian cat.'

'But how does that differ from any other cat?'

'You will soon see that,' said he, laughing. 'Will you kindly draw that shutter and look through?'

I did so, and found that I was gazing into a large, empty room, with stone flags, and small, barred windows upon the farther wall. In the centre of this room, lying in the middle of a golden patch of sunlight, there was stretched a huge creature, as large as a tiger, but as black and sleek as ebony. It was simply a very enormous and very well-kept black cat, and it cuddled up and basked in that yellow pool of light exactly as a cat would do. It was so graceful, so **sinewy**, and so gently and smoothly diabolical, that I could not take my eyes from the opening.

'Isn't he splendid?' said my host, enthusiastically.

'Glorious! I never saw such a noble creature.'

'Some people call it a black puma, but really it is not a puma at all. That fellow is nearly eleven feet from tail to tip. Four years ago he was a little ball of black fluff, with two yellow eyes staring out of it. He was sold me as a new-born cub up in the wild country at the head-waters of the Rio Negro. They speared his mother to death after she had killed a dozen of them.'

'They are ferocious, then?'

'The most absolutely treacherous and bloodthirsty creatures upon earth. You talk about a Brazilian cat to an up-country Indian, and see him get the jumps. They prefer humans to game. This fellow has never tasted living blood yet, but when he does he will be a terror. At present he won't stand anyone but me in his den. Even Baldwin, the groom, dare not go near him. As to me, I am his mother and father in one.'

As he spoke he suddenly, to my astonishment, opened the door and slipped in, closing it instantly behind him. At the sound of his voice the huge, lithe creature rose, yawned and rubbed its round, black head affectionately against his side, while he patted and fondled it.

---

sinewy muscular, strong

'Now, Tommy, into your cage!' said he.

The monstrous cat walked over to one side of the room and coiled itself up under a grating. Everard King came out, and taking the iron handle which I have mentioned, he began to turn it. As he did so the line of bars in the corridor began to pass through a slot in the wall and closed up the front of this grating, so as to make an effective cage. When it was in position, he opened the door once more and invited me into the room, which was heavy with the pungent, musty smell peculiar to the great carnivora.

'That's how we work it,' said he. 'We give him the run of the room for exercise, and then at night we put him in his cage. You can let him out by turning the handle from the passage, or you can, as you have seen, coop him up in the same way. No, no, you should not do that!'

I had put my hand between the bars to pat the glossy, heaving flank. He pulled it back, with a serious face.

'I assure you that he is not safe. Don't imagine that because I can take liberties with him anyone else can. He is very exclusive in his friends – aren't you, Tommy? Ah, he hears his lunch coming to him! Don't you, boy?'

A step had sounded in the stone-flagged passage and the creature had sprung to his feet and was pacing up and down the narrow cage, his yellow eyes gleaming and his scarlet tongue rippling and quivering over the white line of his jagged teeth. A groom entered with a coarse joint upon a tray, and thrust it through the bars to him. He pounced lightly upon it, carried it off to the corner, and there, holding it between his paws, tore and wrenched at it, raising his bloody muzzle every now and then to look at us. It was a **malignant** and yet fascinating sight.

---

malignant evil-looking

'You can't wonder that I am fond of him, can you?' said my host, as we left the room, 'especially when you consider that I have had the rearing of him. It was no joke bringing him over from the centre of South America; but here he is safe and sound – and, as I have said, far the most perfect specimen in Europe. The people at the Zoo are dying to have him, but I really can't part with him. Now, I think that I have inflicted my hobby upon you long enough, so we cannot do better than follow Tommy's example, and go to our lunch.'

My South American relative was so engrossed by his grounds and their curious occupants, that I hardly gave him credit at first for having any interests outside them. That he had some, and pressing ones, was soon borne in upon me by the number of telegrams which he received. They arrived at all hours, and were always opened by him with the utmost eagerness and anxiety upon his face. Sometimes I imagined that it must be the Turf, and sometimes the Stock Exchange, but certainly he had some very urgent business going forward which was not transacted upon the downs of Suffolk. During the six days of my visit he had never fewer than three or four telegrams a day, and sometimes as many as seven or eight.

I had occupied these six days so well, that by the end of them I had succeeded in getting upon the most cordial terms with my cousin. Every night we had sat up late in the billiard-room, he telling me the most extraordinary stories of his adventures in America – stories so desperate and reckless, that I could hardly associate them with the brown little chubby man before me. In return, I ventured upon some of my own reminiscences of London life, which interested him so much that he vowed he would come up to Grosvenor Mansions and stay with me. He was anxious to see the faster side of city life, and certainly, though I say it, he could not have chosen a more competent guide. It was not until the last day of my visit that I ventured to approach that which was on my mind. I told him frankly about my **pecuniary** difficulties and my impending ruin, and I asked his advice – though I hoped for something more solid. He listened attentively, puffing hard at his cigar.

'But surely,' said he, 'you are the heir of our relative, Lord Southerton?'

'I have every reason to believe so, but he would never make me any allowance.'

'No, no, I have heard of his miserly ways. My poor Marshall, your position has been a very hard one. By the way, have you heard any news of Lord Southerton's health lately?'

'He has always been in a critical condition ever since my childhood.'

'Exactly – a creaking hinge, if ever there was one. Your inheritance may be a long way off. Dear me, how awkwardly situated you are!'

'I had some hopes, sir, that you, knowing all the facts, might be inclined to advance –'

'Don't say another word, my dear boy,' he cried, with the utmost cordiality; 'we shall talk it over tonight, and I give you my word that whatever is in my power shall be done.'

I was not sorry that my visit was drawing to a close, for it is unpleasant to feel that there is one person in the house who eagerly desires your departure. Mrs King's sallow face and forbidding eyes had become more and more hateful to me. She was no longer actively rude – her fear of her husband prevented her – but she pushed her insane jealousy to the extent of ignoring me, never addressing me, and in every way making my stay at Greylands as uncomfortable as she could. So offensive was her

pecuniary financial

manner during that last day, that I should certainly have left had it not been for that interview with my host in the evening which would, I hoped, retrieve my broken fortunes.

It was very late when it occurred, for my relative, who had been receiving even more telegrams than usual during the day, went off to his study after dinner and only emerged when the household had retired to bed. I heard him go round locking the doors, as his custom was of a night, and finally he joined me in the billiard-room. His stout figure was wrapped in a dressing-gown and he wore a pair of red Turkish slippers without any heels. Settling down into an armchair, he brewed himself a glass of grog, in which I could not help noticing that the whisky considerably predominated over the water.

'My word!' said he, 'what a night!'

It was, indeed. The wind was howling and screaming round the house, and the latticed windows rattled and shook as if they were coming in. The glow of the yellow lamps and the flavour of our cigars seemed the brighter and more fragrant for the contrast.

'Now, my boy,' said my host, 'we have the house and the night to ourselves. Let me have an idea of how your affairs stand, and I will see what can be done to set them in order. I wish to hear every detail.'

Thus encouraged, I entered into a long **exposition**, in which all my tradesmen and creditors, from my landlord to my valet, figured in turn. I had notes in my pocket-book and I marshalled my facts and gave, I flatter myself, a very businesslike statement of my own unbusinesslike ways and lamentable position. I was depressed, however, to notice that my companion's eyes were vacant and his attention elsewhere. When he did occasionally throw out a remark it was so entirely perfunctory and pointless,

---

exposition a description or explanation

that I was sure he had not in the least followed my remarks. Every now and then he roused himself and put on some show of interest, asking me to repeat or to explain more fully, but it was always to sink once more into the same brown study. At last he rose and threw the end of his cigar into the grate.

'I'll tell you what, my boy,' said he. 'I never had a head for figures, so you will excuse me. You must jot it all down upon paper, and let me have a note of the amount. I'll understand it when I see it in black and white.'

The proposal was encouraging. I promised to do so.

'And now it's time we were in bed. By Jove, there's one o'clock striking in the hall.'

The tingling of the chiming clock broke through the deep roar of the gale. The wind was sweeping past with the rush of a great river.

'I must see my cat before I go to bed,' said my host. 'A high wind excites him. Will you come?'

'Certainly,' said I.

'Then tread softly and don't speak, for everyone is asleep.'

We passed quietly down the lamp-lit Persian-rugged hall, and through the door at the farther end. All was dark in the stone corridor, but a stable lantern hung on a hook, and my host took it down and lit it. There was no grating visible in the passage, so I knew that the beast was in its cage.

'Come in!' said my relative, and opened the door.

A deep growling as we entered showed that the storm had really excited the creature. In the flickering light of the lantern, we saw it, a huge black mass coiled in the corner of its den and throwing a squat, **uncouth** shadow upon the whitewashed wall. Its tail switched angrily among the straw.

---

uncouth uncivilised, wild

'Poor Tommy is not in the best of tempers,' said Everard King, holding up the lantern and looking in at him. 'What a black devil he looks, doesn't he? I must give him a little supper to put him in a better humour. Would you mind holding the lantern for a moment?'

I took it from his hand and he stepped to the door.

'His larder is just outside here,' said he. 'You will excuse me for an instant, won't you?' He passed out, and the door shut with a sharp metallic click behind him.

That hard crisp sound made my heart stand still. A sudden wave of terror passed over me. A vague perception of some monstrous treachery turned me cold. I sprang to the door, but there was no handle upon the inner side.

'Here!' I cried. 'Let me out!'

'All right! Don't make a row!' said my host from the passage. 'You've got the light all right.'

'Yes, but I don't care about being locked in alone like this.'

'Don't you?' I heard his hearty, chuckling laugh. 'You won't be alone long.'

'Let me out, sir!' I repeated angrily. 'I tell you I don't allow practical jokes of this sort.'

'Practical is the word,' said he, with another hateful chuckle. And then suddenly I heard, amidst the roar of the storm, the creak and whine of the winch-handle turning and the rattle of the grating as it passed through the slot. Great God, he was letting loose the Brazilian cat!

In the light of the lantern I saw the bars sliding slowly before me. Already there was an opening a foot wide at the farther end. With a scream I seized the last bar with my hands and pulled with the strength of a madman. I was a madman with rage and horror. For, a minute or more I held the thing motionless. I knew that he was straining with all his force upon the handle and that the leverage was sure to overcome me. I gave inch by inch, my feet sliding along the stones, and all the time I begged and prayed this inhuman monster to save me from this horrible death. I **conjured** him by his kinship. I reminded him that I was his guest; I begged to know what harm I had ever done him. His only answers were the tugs and jerks upon the handle, each of which, in spite of all my struggles, pulled another bar through the opening. Clinging and clutching, I was dragged across the whole front of the cage, until at last, with aching wrists and lacerated fingers, I gave up the hopeless struggle. The grating clanged back as I released it, and an instant later I heard the shuffle of the Turkish slippers in the passage, and the slam of the distant door. Then everything was silent.

The creature had never moved during this time. He lay still in the corner, and his tail had ceased switching. This apparition of a man adhering to his bars and dragged screaming across him had apparently filled him with amazement. I saw his great eyes staring steadily at me. I had dropped the lantern when I seized the bars, but it still burned upon the floor, and I made a movement to grasp it, with some idea that its light might protect me. But the instant I moved, the beast gave a deep and menacing growl. I stopped and stood still, quivering with fear in every limb. The cat (if one may call so fearful a creature by so homely a name) was not more than ten feet from me. The eyes glimmered like two disks of phosphorus in the darkness. They appalled and yet fascinated me. I could not take my own eyes from them. Nature plays strange tricks with us at such moments of intensity, and those glimmering lights waxed and waned with a steady rise and fall. Sometimes they seemed to be tiny points of extreme brilliancy – little electric sparks in the black obscurity – then they would widen and widen until all that corner of the room was

---

conjured begged

filled with their shifting and sinister light. And then suddenly they went out altogether.

The beast had closed its eyes. I do not know whether there may be any truth in the old idea of the dominance of the human gaze, or whether the huge cat was simply drowsy, but the fact remains that, far from showing any symptom of attacking me, it simply rested its sleek, black head upon its huge forepaws and seemed to sleep. I stood, fearing to move lest I should rouse it into malignant life once more. But at least I was able to think clearly now that the baleful eyes were off me. Here I was shut up for the night with the ferocious beast. My own instincts, to say nothing of the words of the **plausible** villain who laid this trap for me, warned me that the animal was as savage as its master. How could I stave it off until morning? The door was hopeless, and so were the narrow, barred windows. There was no shelter anywhere in the bare, stone-flagged room. To cry for assistance was absurd. I knew that this den was an outhouse, and that the corridor which connected it with the house was at least a hundred feet long. Besides, with that gale thundering outside, my cries were not likely to be heard. I had only my own courage and my own wits to trust to.

And then, with a fresh wave of horror, my eyes fell upon the lantern. The candle had burned low, and was already beginning to gutter. In ten minutes it would be out. I had only ten minutes then in which to do something, for I felt that if I were once left in the dark with that fearful beast I should be incapable of action. The very thought of it paralysed me. I cast my despairing eyes round this chamber of death, and they rested upon one spot which seemed to promise I will not say safety, but less immediate and imminent danger than the open floor.

---

plausible reasonable-sounding

I have said that the cage had a top as well as a front, and this top was left standing when the front was wound through the slot in the wall. It consisted of bars at a few inches' interval, with stout wire netting between, and it rested upon a strong **stanchion** at each end. It stood now as a great barred canopy over the crouching figure in the corner. The space between this iron shelf and the roof may have been from two to three feet. If I could only get up there, squeezed in between bars and ceiling, I should have only one vulnerable side. I should be safe from below, from behind, and from each side. Only on the open face of it could I be attacked. There, it is true, I had no protection whatever; but at least I should be out of the brute's path when he began to pace about his den. He would have to come out of his way to reach me. It was now or never, for once the light were out it would be impossible. With a gulp in my throat I sprang up, seized the iron edge of the top, and swung myself panting on to it. I writhed in, face downwards, and found myself looking straight into the terrible eyes and yawning jaws of the cat. Its fetid breath came up into my face like the steam from some foul pot.

It appeared, however, to be rather curious than angry. With a sleek ripple of its long black back it rose, stretched itself, and then rearing itself on its hind legs, with one forepaw against the wall, it raised the other and drew its claws across the wire meshes beneath me. One sharp, white hook tore through my trousers – for I may mention that I was still in evening dress – and dug a furrow in my knee. It was not meant as an attack, but rather as an experiment, for upon my giving a sharp cry of pain he dropped down again, and springing lightly into the room, he began walking swiftly round it, looking up every now and again in my direction. For my part I shuffled backwards until I lay with my back against the

---

stanchion supporting bar

wall, screwing myself into the smallest space possible. The farther I got the more difficult it was for him to attack me.

He seemed more excited now that he had begun to move about, and he ran swiftly and noiselessly round and round the den, passing continually underneath the iron couch upon which I lay. It was wonderful to see so great a bulk passing like a shadow, with hardly the softest thudding of velvety pads. The candle was burning low – so low that I could hardly see the creature. And then, with a last flare and splutter, it went out altogether. I was alone with the cat in the dark!

It helps one to face a danger when one knows that one has done all that possibly can be done. There is nothing for it then but to quietly await the result. In this case, there was no chance of safety anywhere except the precise spot where I was. I stretched myself out, therefore, and lay silently, almost breathlessly, hoping that the beast might forget my presence if I did nothing to remind him. I reckoned that it must already be two o'clock. At four it would be full dawn. I had not more than two hours to wait for daylight.

Outside, the storm was still raging, and the rain lashed continually against the little windows. Inside, the poisonous and fetid air was overpowering. I could neither hear nor see the cat. I tried to think about other things – but only one had power enough to draw my mind from my terrible position. That was the contemplation of my cousin's villainy, his unparalleled hypocrisy, his malignant hatred of me. Beneath that cheerful face there lurked the spirit of a medieval assassin. And as I thought of it I saw more clearly how cunningly the thing had been arranged. He had apparently gone to bed with the others. No doubt he had his witnesses to prove it. Then, unknown to them, he had slipped down, had lured me into this den and abandoned me. His story would be so simple. He had left me to finish my cigar in the billiard-room. I had gone down on my own account to have a last look at the cat. I had entered the room without observing that the cage was opened, and I had been caught. How could such a crime be brought home to him? Suspicion, perhaps – but proof, never!

How slowly those dreadful two hours went by! Once I heard a low, rasping sound, which I took to be the creature licking its own fur. Several times those greenish eyes gleamed at me through the darkness, but never in a fixed stare, and my hopes grew stronger that my presence had been forgotten or ignored. At last the least faint glimmer of light came through the windows – I first dimly saw them as two grey squares upon the black wall, then grey turned to white, and I could see my terrible companion once more. And he, alas, could see me!

It was evident to me at once that he was in a much more dangerous and aggressive mood than when I had seen him last. The cold of the morning had irritated him, and he was hungry as well. With a continual growl he paced swiftly up and down the side of the room which was farthest from my refuge, his whiskers bristling angrily and his tail switching and lashing. As he turned at the corners his savage eyes always looked upwards at me with a dreadful menace. I knew then that he meant to kill me. Yet I found myself even at that moment admiring the sinuous grace of the devilish thing, its long, undulating, rippling movements, the gloss of its beautiful flanks, the vivid, palpitating scarlet of the glistening tongue which hung from the jet-black muzzle. And all the time that deep, threatening growl was rising and rising in an unbroken crescendo. I knew that the crisis was at hand.

It was a miserable hour to meet such a death – so cold, so comfortless, shivering in my light dress clothes upon this gridiron of torment upon which I was stretched. I tried to brace myself to it, to raise my soul above it, and at the same time, with the

lucidity which comes to a perfectly desperate man, I cast round for some possible means of escape. One thing was clear to me. If that front of the cage was only back in its position once more, I could find a sure refuge behind it. Could I possibly pull it back? I hardly dared to move for fear of bringing the creature upon me. Slowly, very slowly, I put my hand forward until it grasped the edge of the front, the final bar which protruded through the wall. To my surprise it came quite easily to my jerk. Of course the difficulty of drawing it out arose from the fact that I was clinging to it. I pulled again, and three inches of it came through. It ran apparently on wheels. I pulled again ... and then the cat sprang!

It was so quick, so sudden, that I never saw it happen. I simply heard the savage snarl and in an instant afterwards the blazing yellow eyes, the flattened black head with its red tongue and flashing teeth, were within reach of me. The impact of the creature shook the bars upon which I lay, until I thought (as far as I could think of anything at such a moment) that they were coming down. The cat swayed there for an instant, the head and front paws quite close to me, the hind paws clawing to find a grip upon the edge of the grating. I heard the claws rasping as they clung to the wire netting and the breath of the beast made me sick. But its bound had been miscalculated. It could not retain its position. Slowly, grinning with rage, and scratching madly at the bars, it swung backwards and dropped heavily upon the floor. With a growl it instantly faced round to me and crouched for another spring.

I knew that the next few moments would decide my fate. The creature had learned by experience. It would not miscalculate again. I must act promptly, fearlessly, if I were to have a chance of life. In an instant I had formed my plan. Pulling off my dress-

---

lucidity the ability to think clearly

coat, I threw it down over the head of the beast. At the same moment I dropped over the edge, seized the end of the front grating, and pulled it frantically out of the wall.

It came more easily than I could have expected. I rushed across the room, bearing it with me; but, as I rushed, the accident of my position put me upon the outer side. Had it been the other way, I might have come off scathless. As it was, there was a moment's pause as I stopped it and tried to pass in through the opening which I had left. That moment was enough to give time to the creature to toss off the coat with which I had blinded him and to spring upon me. I hurled myself through the gap and pulled the rails to behind me, but he seized my leg before I could entirely withdraw it. One stroke of that huge paw tore off my calf as a shaving of wood curls off before a plane. The next moment, bleeding and fainting, I was lying among the foul straw with a line of friendly bars between me and the creature which ramped so frantically against them.

Too wounded to move and too faint to be conscious of fear, I could only lie, more dead than alive, and watch it. It pressed its broad, black chest against the bars and angled for me with its crooked paws as I have seen a kitten do before a mousetrap. It ripped my clothes, but, stretch as it would, it could not quite reach me. I have heard of the curious numbing effect produced by wounds from the great carnivora, and now I was destined to experience it, for I had lost all sense of personality and was as interested in the cat's failure or success as if it were some game which I was watching. And then gradually my mind drifted away into strange vague dreams, always with that black face and red tongue coming back into them, and so I lost myself in the nirvana of delirium, the blessed relief of those who are too sorely tried.

Tracing the course of events afterwards, I conclude that I must have been insensible for about two hours. What roused me to consciousness once more was that sharp metallic click which had been the precursor of my terrible experience. It was the shooting back of the spring lock. Then, before my senses were clear enough entirely to apprehend what they saw, I was aware of the round, benevolent face of my cousin peering in through the open door. What he saw evidently amazed him. There was the cat crouching on the floor. I was stretched upon my back in my shirtsleeves within the cage, my trousers torn to ribbons and a great pool of blood all round me. I can see his amazed face now, with the morning sunlight upon it. He peered at me, and peered again. Then he closed the door behind him, and advanced to the cage to see if I were really dead.

I cannot undertake to say what happened. I was not in a fit state to witness or to chronicle such events. I can only say that I was suddenly conscious that his face was away from me – that he was looking towards the animal.

'Good old Tommy!' he cried. 'Good old Tommy!'

Then he came near the bars, with his back still towards me.

'Down, you stupid beast!' he roared. 'Down, sir! Don't you know your master?'

Suddenly even in my bemuddled brain a remembrance came of those words of his when he had said that the taste of blood would turn the cat into a fiend. My blood had done it, but he was to pay the price.

'Get away!' he screamed. 'Get away, you devil! Baldwin! Baldwin! Oh, my God!'

And then I heard him fall, and rise, and fall again, with a sound like the ripping of sacking. His screams grew fainter until they were lost in the worrying snarl. And then, after I thought that he was dead, I saw, as in a nightmare, a blinded, tattered, blood-soaked figure running wildly round the room – and that was the last glimpse I had of him before I fainted once again.

I was many months in my recovery – in fact, I cannot say that I have ever recovered, for to the end of my days I shall carry a stick as a sign of my night with the Brazilian cat. Baldwin, the groom, and the other servants could not tell what had occurred, when, drawn by the death-cries of their master, they found me behind the bars, and his remains – or what they afterwards discovered to be his remains – in the clutch of the creature which he had reared. They stalled him off with hot irons, and afterwards shot him through the loophole of the door before they could finally extricate me. I was carried to my bedroom, and there, under the roof of my would-be murderer, I remained between life and death for several weeks. They had sent for a surgeon from Clipton and a nurse from London, and in a month I was able to be carried to the station, and so conveyed back once more to Grosvenor Mansions.

I have one remembrance of that illness, which might have been part of the ever-changing panorama conjured up by a delirious brain were it not so definitely fixed in my memory. One night, when the nurse was absent, the door of my chamber opened and a tall woman in blackest mourning slipped into the room. She came across to me and as she bent her sallow face I saw by the faint gleam of the nightlight that it was the Brazilian woman whom my cousin had married. She staked intently into my face, and her expression was more kindly than I had ever seen it.

'Are you conscious?' she asked.

I feebly nodded – for I was still very weak.

'Well, then, I only wished to say to you that you have yourself to blame. Did I not do all I could for you? From the beginning I tried to drive you from the house. By every means, short of betraying my husband, I tried to save you from him. I knew that he had a reason for bringing you here. I knew that he would never let you get away again. No one knew him as I knew him, who had suffered from him so often. I did not dare to tell you all this. He would have killed me. But I did my best for you. As things have turned out, you have been the best friend that I have ever had. You have set me free, and I fancied that nothing but death would do that. I am sorry if you are hurt, but I cannot reproach myself. I told you that you were a fool – and a fool you have been.' She crept out of the room, the bitter, singular woman, and I was never destined to see her again. With what remained from her husband's property she went back to her native land, and I have heard that she afterwards took the veil at Pernambuco.

It was not until I had been back in London for some time that the doctors pronounced me to be well enough to do business. It was not a very welcome permission to me, for I feared that it would be the signal for an inrush of creditors; but it was Summers, my lawyer, who first took advantage of it.

'I am very glad to see that your lordship is so much better,' said he. 'I have been waiting a long time to offer my congratulations.'

'What do you mean, Summers? This is no time for joking.'

'I mean what I say,' he answered. 'You have been Lord Southerton for the last six weeks, but we feared that it would retard your recovery if you were to learn it.'

Lord Southerton! One of the richest peers in England! I could not believe my ears. And then suddenly I thought of the time which had elapsed, and how it coincided with my injuries.

'Then Lord Southerton must have died about the same time that I was hurt?'

'His death occurred upon that very day.' Summers looked hard at me as I spoke, and I am convinced – for he was a very shrewd fellow – that he had guessed the true state of the case. He paused for a moment as if awaiting a confidence from me, but I could not see what was to be gained by exposing such a family scandal.

'Yes, a very curious coincidence,' he continued, with the same knowing look, 'Of course, you are aware that your cousin Everard King was the next heir to the estates. Now, if it had been you instead of him who had been torn to pieces by this tiger, or whatever it was, then of course he would have been Lord Southerton at the present moment.'

'No doubt,' said I.

'And he took such an interest in it,' said Summers. 'I happen to know that the late Lord Southerton's valet was in his pay, and that he used to have telegrams from him every few hours to tell him how he was getting on. That would be about the time when you were down there. Was it not strange that he should wish to be so well informed, since he knew that he was not the direct heir?'

'Very strange,' said I. 'And now, Summers, if you will bring me my bills and a new chequebook, we will begin to get things into order.'

To Build a Fire
Jack London

Day had broken cold and grey, exceedingly cold and grey, when the man turned aside from the main Yukon trail and climbed the high earth-bank, where a dim and little-travelled trail led eastward through the fat spruce timberland. It was a steep bank, and he paused for breath at the top, excusing the act to himself by looking at his watch. It was nine o'clock. There was no sun nor hint of sun, though there was not a cloud in the sky. It was a clear day, and yet there seemed an intangible pall over the face of things, a subtle gloom that made the day dark, and that was due to the absence of sun. This fact did not worry the man. He was used to the lack of sun. It had been days since he had seen the sun, and he knew that a few more days must pass before that cheerful orb, due south, would just peep above the skyline and dip immediately from view.

The man flung a look back along the way he had come. The Yukon lay a mile wide and hidden under three feet of ice. On top of this ice were as many feet of snow. It was all pure white, rolling in gentle undulations where the ice-jams of the freeze-up had formed. North and south, as far as his eye could see, it was unbroken white, save for a dark hair-line that curved and twisted from around the sprucecovered island to the south, and that curved and twisted away into the north, where it disappeared behind another spruce-covered island. This dark hair-line was the trail – the main trail – that led south five hundred miles to the Chilcoot Pass, Dyea, and salt water; and that led north seventy miles to Dawson, and still on to the north a thousand miles to Nulato, and finally to St Michael on Bering Sea, a thousand miles and half a thousand more.

But all this – the mysterious, far-reaching hair-line trail, the absence of sun from the sky, the tremendous cold, and the strangeness and weirdness of it all – made no impression on the man. It was not because he was long used to it. He was a new-comer in the land, a *chechaquo*, and this was his first winter. The trouble with him was that he was without imagination. He was quick and alert in the things of life, but only in the things, and not in the significances. Fifty degrees below zero meant eighty-odd degrees of frost. Such fact impressed him as being cold and uncomfortable, and that was all. It did not lead him to meditate upon his frailty as a creature of temperature, and upon man's frailty in general, able only to live within certain narrow limits of heat and cold; and from there on it did not lead him to the conjectural field of immortality and man's place in the universe. Fifty degrees below zero stood for a bite of frost that hurt and that must be guarded against by the use of mittens, ear-flaps, warm moccasins, and thick socks. Fifty degrees below zero was to him just precisely fifty degrees below zero. That there should be anything more to it than that was a thought that never entered his head.

As he turned to go on, he spat speculatively. There was a sharp, explosive crackle that startled him. He spat again. And again, in the air, before it could fall to the snow, the spittle crackled. He knew that at fifty below spittle crackled on the snow, but this spittle had crackled in the air. Undoubtedly it was colder than fifty below – how much colder he did not know. But the temperature did not matter. He was bound for the old claim on the left fork of Henderson Creek, where the boys were already. They had come over across the divide from the Indian Creek country, while he had come the roundabout way to take a look at the possibilities of getting out logs in the spring from the islands in the Yukon. He would be in to camp by six o'clock; a bit after dark, it was true, but the boys would be there, a fire would be going, and a hot supper would be ready. As for lunch, he pressed his hand against the protruding bundle under his jacket. It was also tinder his shirt, wrapped up in a handkerchief, and lying against the naked skin. It was the only way to keep the biscuits from freezing. He smiled agreeably to himself as he thought of those biscuits, each cut open and sopped in bacon grease, and each enclosing a generous slice of fried bacon.

He plunged in among the big spruce trees. The trail was faint. A foot of snow had fallen since the last sled had passed over, and he was glad he was without a sled, travelling light. In fact, he carried nothing but the lunch wrapped in the handkerchief. He was surprised, however, at the cold. It certainly was cold, he concluded, as he rubbed his numbed nose and cheek-bones with his mittened hand. He was a warm-whiskered man, but the hair on his face did not protect the high cheek-bones and the eager nose that thrust itself aggressively into the frosty air.

At the man's heels trotted a dog, a big native husky, the proper wolf-dog, grey-coated and without any visible or temperamental difference from its brother, the wild wolf. The animal was depressed by the tremendous cold. It knew that it was no time for travelling. Its instinct told it a truer tale than was told to the man by the man's judgment. In reality, it was not merely colder than fifty below zero; it was colder than sixty below, than seventy below. It was seventy-five below zero. Since the freezing-point is thirty-two above zero it meant that one hundred and seven degrees of frost obtained. The dog did not know anything about thermometers. Possibly in its brain there was no sharp consciousness of a condition of very cold such as was in the man's brain. But the brute had its instinct. It experienced a vague but menacing apprehension that subdued it and made it slink along at the man's heels, and that made it question eagerly every unwonted movement of the man as if expecting him to go into camp or to seek shelter somewhere and build a fire. The dog had learned fire, and it wanted fire, or else to burrow under the snow and cuddle its warmth away from the air.

The frozen moisture of its breathing had settled on its fur in a fine powder of frost, and especially were its jowls, muzzle, and eyelashes whitened by its crystalled breath. The man's red beard and moustache were like-wise frosted, but more solidly, the deposit taking the form of ice and increasing with every warm, moist breath he exhaled. Also, the man was chewing tobacco, and the muzzle of ice held his lips so rigidly that he was unable to clear his chin when he expelled the juice. The result was that a crystal beard of the colour and solidity of amber was increasing its length on his chin. If he fell down it would shatter itself, like glass, into brittle fragments. But he did not mind the appendage. It was the penalty all tobacco-chewers paid in that country, and he had been out before in two cold snaps. They had not been so cold as this, he knew, but by the spirit thermometer at Sixty Mile he knew they had been registered at fifty below and at fifty-five.

He held on through the level stretch of woods for several miles, crossed a wide flat of nigger-heads, and dropped down a bank to the frozen bed of a small stream. This was Henderson Creek, and he knew he was ten miles from the forks. He looked at his watch. It was ten o'clock. He was making four miles an hour, and he calculated that he would arrive at the forks at half-past twelve. He decided to celebrate that event by eating his lunch there.

The dog dropped in again at his heels, with a tail drooping discouragement, as the man swung along the creek-bed. The furrow of the old sled-trail was plainly visible, but a dozen inches of snow covered the marks of the last runners. In a month no man had come up or down that silent creek. The man held steadily on. He was not much given to thinking, and just then particularly he had nothing to think about save that he would eat lunch at the forks and that at six o'clock he would be in camp with the boys. There was nobody to talk to; and, had there been, speech would have been impossible because of the ice-muzzle on his mouth. So he continued monotonously to chew tobacco and to increase the length of his amber beard.

Once in a while the thought reiterated itself that it was very cold and that he had never experienced such cold. As he walked along he rubbed his cheek-bones and nose with the back of his mittened hand. He did this automatically, now and again changing hands. But rub as he would, the instant he stopped his cheek-bones went numb, and the following instant the end of his nose went numb. He was sure to frost his cheeks; he knew that, and experienced a pang of regret that he had not devised a nose-strap of the sort Bud wore in cold snaps. Such a strap passed across the cheeks, as well, and saved them. But it didn't matter much, after all. What were frosted cheeks? A bit painful, that was all; they were never serious.

Empty as the man's mind was of thoughts, he was keenly observant, and he noticed the changes in the creek, the curves and bends and timber-jams, and always he sharply noted where he placed his feet. Once, coming around a bend, he shied abruptly, like a startled horse, curved away from the place where he had been walking, and retreated several paces back along the trail. The creek he knew was frozen clear to the bottom – no creek could contain water in that arctic winter – but he knew also that there were springs that bubbled out from the hillsides and ran along under the snow and on top the ice of the creek. He knew that the coldest snaps never froze these springs, and he knew likewise their danger. They were traps. They hid pools of water under the snow that might be three inches deep, or three feet.

Sometimes a skin of ice half an inch thick covered them, and in turn was covered by the snow. Sometimes there were alternate layers of water and ice-skin, so that when one broke through he kept on breaking through for a while, sometimes wetting himself to the waist.

That was why he had shied in such panic. He had felt the ice give under his feet and heard the crackle of a snow-hidden ice-skin. And to get his feet wet in such a temperature meant trouble and danger. At the very least it meant delay, for he would be forced to stop and build a fire, and under its protection to bare his feet while he dried his socks and moccasins. He stood and studied the creek-bed and its banks, and decided that the flow of water came from the right. He reflected awhile, rubbing his nose and cheeks and skirted to the left, stepping gingerly and testing the footing for each step. Once clear of the danger, he took a fresh chew of tobacco and swung along at his four-mile gait.

In the course of the next two hours he came upon several similar traps. Usually the snow above the hidden pools had a sunken, candied appearance that advertised the danger. Once again, however, he had a close call; and once, suspecting danger, he compelled the dog to go on in front. The dog did not want to go. It hung back until the man shoved it forward, and then it went quickly across the white, unbroken surface. Suddenly it broke through, floundered to one side, and got away to firmer footing. It had wet its forefeet and legs and almost immediately the water that clung to it turned to ice. It made quick efforts to lick the ice off its legs, then dropped down in the snow and began to bite out the ice that had formed between the toes. This was a matter of instinct. To permit the ice to remain would mean sore feet. It did not know this. It merely obeyed the mysterious prompting that arose from the deep crypts of its being. But the man knew, having achieved a judgment on the subject, and he removed the mitten from his right hand and helped tear out the ice-particles. He did not expose his fingers more than a minute and was astonished at the swift numbness that smote them. It certainly was cold. He pulled on the mitten hastily, and beat the hand savagely across his chest.

At twelve o'clock the day was at its brightest. Yet the sun was too far south on its winter journey to clear the horizon. The bulge of the earth intervened between it and Henderson Creek, where the man walked under a clear sky at noon and cast no shadow. At half-past twelve, to the minute, he arrived at the forks of the creek. He was pleased at the speed he had made. If he kept it up, he would certainly be with the boys by six. He unbuttoned his jacket and shirt and drew forth his lunch. The action consumed no more than a quarter of a minute, yet in that brief moment the numbness laid hold of the exposed fingers. He did not put the mitten on, but, instead, struck the fingers a dozen sharp smashes against his leg. Then he sat down on a snow-covered log to eat. The sting that followed upon the striking of his fingers against his leg ceased so quickly that he was startled. He had had no chance to take a bite of biscuit. He struck the fingers repeatedly and returned them to the mitten, baring the other hand for the purpose, of eating. He tried to take a mouthful but the ice-muzzle prevented. He had forgotten to build a fire and thaw out. He chuckled at his foolishness, and as he chuckled he noted the numbness creeping into the exposed fingers. Also, he noted that the stinging which had first come to his toes when he sat down was already passing away. He wondered whether the toes were warm or numbed. He moved them inside the moccasins and decided that they were numbed.

He pulled the mitten on hurriedly and stood up. He was a bit frightened. He stamped up and down until the stinging returned into the feet. It certainly was cold was his thought. That man from Sulphur Creek had spoken the truth when telling how cold it sometimes got in the country. And he had laughed at him at the time! That showed one must not be too sure of things. There was no mistake about it, it *was* cold. He strode up and down, stamping his feet and threshing his arms, until reassured by the returning warmth. Then he got out matches and proceeded to make a fire. From the undergrowth, where high water of the previous spring had lodged a supply of seasoned twigs, he got his firewood. Working carefully from a small beginning, he soon had a roaring fire, over which he thawed the ice from his face and in the protection of which he ate his biscuits. For the moment the cold of space was outwitted. The dog took satisfaction in the fire, stretching out close enough for warmth and far enough away to escape being singed.

When the man had finished, he filled his pipe and took his comfortable time over a smoke. Then he pulled on his mittens, settled the ear-flaps of his cap firmly about his ears, and took the creek trail up the left fork. The dog was disappointed and yearned back towards the fire. This man did not know cold. Possibly all the generations of his ancestry had been ignorant of cold, of real cold, of cold one hundred and seven degrees below freezing-point. But the dog knew; all its ancestry knew, and it had inherited the knowledge. And it knew that it was not good to walk abroad in such fearful cold. It was the time to lie snug in a hole in the snow and wait for a curtain of cloud to be drawn across the face of outer space whence this cold came. On the other hand, there was no keen intimacy between the dog and the man. The one was the toil-slave of the other, and the only caresses it had ever received were the caresses of the whip-lash and of harsh and menacing throat-sounds that threatened the whip-lash. So the dog made no effort to communicate its apprehension to the man. It was not concerned in the welfare of the man; it was for its own sake that it yearned back towards the fire. But the man whistled, and spoke to it with the sound of whip-lashes, and the dog swung in at the man's heels and followed after.

The man took a chew of tobacco and proceeded to start a new amber beard. Also, his moist breath quickly powdered with white his moustache, eyebrows, and lashes. There did not seem to be so many springs on the left fork of the Henderson, and for half an hour the man saw no signs of any. And then it happened. At a place where there were no signs, where the soft, unbroken snow seemed to advertise solidity beneath, the man broke through. It was not deep. He wet himself halfway to the knees before he floundered out to the firm crust.

He was angry, and cursed his luck aloud. He had hoped to get into camp with the boys at six o'clock, and this would delay him an hour, for he would have to build a fire and dry out his footgear. This was imperative at that low temperature – he knew that much; and he turned aside to the bank, which he climbed. On top, tangled in the underbrush about the trunks of several small spruce trees, was a high-water deposit of dry fire-wood – sticks and twigs, principally, but also larger portions of seasoned branches and fine, dry, last year's grasses. He threw down several large pieces on top of the snow. This served for a foundation and prevented the young flame from drowning itself in the snow it otherwise would melt. The flame he got by touching a match to a small shred of birch-bark that he took from his pocket. This burned even more readily than paper. Placing it on the foundation, he fed the young flames with wisps of dry grass and with the tiniest dry twigs.

He worked slowly and carefully, keenly aware of his danger. Gradually, as the flame grew stronger, he increased the size of the twigs with which he fed it. He squatted in the snow, pulling the twigs out from their entanglement in the brush and feeding directly to the flame. He knew there must be no failure. When it is seventy-five below zero, a man must not fail in his first attempt to build a fire – that is, if his feet are wet. If his feet are dry, and he fails, he can run along the trail for half a mile and restore his circulation. But the circulation of wet and freezing feet cannot be restored by running when it is seventy-five below. No matter how fast he runs, the wet feet will freeze the harder.

All this the man knew. The old-timer on Sulphur Creek had told him about it the previous fall, and now he was appreciating the advice. Already all sensation had gone out of his feet. To build the fire he had been forced to remove his mittens, and the fingers had quickly gone numb. His pace of four miles an hour had kept his heart pumping blood to the surface of his body and to all the extremities. But the instant he stopped, the action of the pump eased down. The cold of space smote the unprotected tip of the planet, and he, being on that unprotected tip, received the full force of the blow. The blood of his body recoiled before it. The blood was alive, like the dog, and like the dog it wanted to hide away and cover itself up from the fearful cold, So long as he walked four miles an hour, he pumped that blood, willy-nilly, to the surface; but now it ebbed away and sank down into the recesses of his body. The extremities were the first to feel its absence. His wet feet froze the faster, and his exposed fingers numbed the faster, though they had not yet begun to freeze. Nose and cheeks were already freezing, while the skin of all his body chilled as it lost its blood.

But he was safe. Toes and nose and cheeks would be only touched by the frost, for the fire was beginning to burn with strength. He was feeding it with twigs the size of his finger. In another minute he would be able to feed it with branches the size of his wrist, and then he could remove his wet footgear, and while it dried he could keep his naked feet warm by the fire, rubbing them at first, of course, with snow. The fire was a success. He was safe. He remembered the advice of the old-timer on Sulphur Creek, and smiled. The old-timer had been very serious in laying down the law that no man must travel alone in the Klondike after fifty below. Well, here he was; he had had an accident; he was alone; and he saved himself. Those old-timers were rather womanish, some of them, he thought. All a man had to do was to keep his head, and he was all right. Any man who was a man could travel alone. But it was surprising, the rapidity with which his cheeks and nose were freezing. And he had not thought his fingers could go lifeless in so short a time. Lifeless they were, for he could scarcely make them move together to grip a twig, and they seemed remote from his body and from him. When he touched a twig, he had to look and see whether or not he had hold of it. The wires were pretty well down between him and his finger-ends.

All of which counted for little. There was the fire, snapping and crackling and promising life with every dancing flame. He started to untie his moccasins. They were coated with ice; the thick German socks were like sheaths of iron halfway to the knees; and the moccasin strings were like rods of steel all twisted and knotted as by some conflagration. For a moment he tugged with his numbed fingers, then, realizing the folly of it, he drew his sheath-knife.

But before he could cut the strings, it happened. It was his own fault or, rather, his mistake. He should not have built the fire under the spruce tree. He should have built it in the open. But it had been easier to pull the twigs from the brush and drop them directly on the fire. Now the tree under which he had done this carried a weight of snow on its boughs. No wind had blown for weeks, and each bough was fully freighted. Each time he had pulled a twig he had communicated a slight agitation to the tree – an imperceptible agitation, so far as he was concerned, but an agitation sufficient to bring about the disaster. High up in the tree one bough capsized its load of snow. This fell on the boughs beneath, capsizing them. This process continued, spreading out and involving the whole tree. It grew like an avalanche, and it descended without warning upon the man and the fire, and the fire was blotted out! Where it had burned was a mantle of fresh and disordered snow.

The man was shocked. It was as though he had just heard his own sentence of death. For a moment he sat and stared at the spot where the fire had been. Then he grew very calm. Perhaps the old-timer on Sulphur Creek was right. If he had only had a trail-mate he would have been in no danger now. The trail-mate could have built the fire. Well, it was up to him to build the fire over again, and this second time there must be no failure. Even if he succeeded, he would most likely lose some toes. His feet must be badly frozen by now, and there would be some time before the second fire was ready.

Such were his thoughts, but he did not sit and think them. He was busy all the time they were passing through his mind. He made a new foundation for a fire, this time in the open, where no treacherous tree could blot it out. Next, he gathered dry grasses and tiny twigs from the high-water flotsam. He could not bring his fingers together to pull them out, but he was able to gather them by the handful. In this way he got many rotten twigs and bits of green moss that were undesirable, but it was the best he could do. He worked methodically, even collecting an armful of the larger branches to be used later when the fire gathered strength. And all the while the dog sat and watched him, a certain yearning wistfulness in its eyes, for it looked upon him as the fire-provider, and the fire was slow in coming.

When all was ready, the man reached in his pocket for a second piece of birch-bark. He knew the bark was there, and, though he could not feel it with his fingers, he could hear its crisp rustling as he fumbled for it. Try as he would, he could not clutch hold of it. And all the time, in his consciousness, was the knowledge that each instant his feet were freezing. This thought tended to put him in a panic, but he fought against it and kept calm. He pulled on his mittens with his teeth, and threshed his arms back and forth, beating his hands with all his might against his sides. He did this sitting down, and he stood up to do it; and all the while the dog sat in the snow, its wolf-brush of a tail curled around warmly over its forefeet, its sharp wolf-ears pricked forward intently as it watched the man. And the man as he beat and threshed with his arms and hands, felt a great surge of envy as he regarded the creature that was warm and secure in its natural covering.

After a time he was aware of the first far-away signals of sensation in his beaten fingers. The faint tingling grew stronger till it evolved into a stinging ache that was excruciating, but which the man hailed with satisfaction. He stripped the mitten from his right hand and fetched forth the birch-bark. The exposed fingers were quickly going numb again. Next he brought out his bunch of sulphur matches. But the tremendous cold had already driven the life out of his fingers. In his effort to separate one match from the others, the whole bunch fell in the snow. He tried to pick it out of the snow, but failed. The dead fingers could neither touch nor clutch. He was very careful. He drove the thought of his freezing feet, and nose, and cheeks, out of his mind, devoting his whole soul to the matches. He watched, using the sense of vision in place of that of touch, and when he saw his fingers on each side the bunch, he closed – that is, he willed to close them, for the wires were down, and the fingers did not obey. He pulled the mitten on the right hand, and beat it fiercely against his knee. Then, with both mittened hands, he scooped the bunch of matches, along with much snow, into his lap. Yet he was no better off.

After much manipulation he managed to get the bunch between the heels of his mittened hands. In this fashion he carried it to his mouth. The ice crackled and snapped when by a violent effort he opened his mouth. He drew the lower jaw in, curled the upper lip out of the way, and scraped the bunch with his upper teeth in order to separate a match. He succeeded in getting one, which he dropped on his lap. He was no better off, He could not pick it up. Then he devised a way. He picked it up in his teeth and scratched it on his leg. Twenty times he scratched before he succeeded in lighting it. As it flamed he held it with his teeth to the birch bark. But the burning brimstone went up his nostrils and into his lungs, causing him to cough spasmodically. The match fell into the snow and went out.

The old-timer on Sulphur Creek was right, he thought in the moment of controlled despair that ensued: after fifty below, a man should travel with a partner. He beat his hands, but failed in exciting any sensation. Suddenly he bared both hands, removing the mittens with his teeth. He caught the whole bunch between the heels of his hands. His arm-muscles not being frozen enabled him to press the hand-heels tightly against the matches. Then he scratched the bunch along his leg. It flared into flame, seventy sulphur matches at once! There was no wind to blow them out. He kept his head to one side to escape the strangling fumes, and held the blazing bunch to the birch-bark. As he so held it, he became aware of sensation in his hand. His flesh was burning. He could smell it. Deep down below the surface he could feel it. The sensation developed into pain that grew acute. And still he endured it, holding the flame of the matches clumsily because his own burning hands were in the way, absorbing most of the flame.

At last, when he could endure no more, he jerked his hands apart. The blazing matches fell sizzling into the snow, but the birch-bark was alight. He began laying dry grasses and the tiniest twigs on the flame. He could not pick and choose, for he had to lift the fuel between the heels of his hands. Small pieces of rotten wood and green moss clung to the twigs, and he bit them off as well as he could with his teeth. He cherished the flame carefully and awkwardly. It meant life, and it must not perish. The withdrawal of blood from the surface of his body now made him begin to shiver, and he grew more awkward. A large piece of moss fell squarely on the little fire. He tried to poke it out with his fingers, but his shivering frame made him poke too far, and he disrupted the nucleus of the little fire, the burning grasses and tiny twigs separating and scattering. He tried to poke them together again, but in spite of the tenseness of the effort, his shivering got away with him, and the twigs were hopelessly scattered. Each twig gushed a puff of smoke and went out. The fire-provider had failed. As he looked apathetically about him, his eyes chanced on the dog, sitting across the ruins of the fire from him, in the snow, making restless, hunching movements, slightly lifting one forefoot and then the other, shifting its weight back and forth on them with wistful eagerness.

The sight of the dog put a wild idea into his head. He remembered the tale of the man, caught in a blizzard, who killed a steer and crawled inside the carcass, and so was saved. He would kill the dog and bury his hands in the warm body until the numbness went out of them. Then he could built another fire. He spoke to the dog, calling it to him; but in his voice was a strange note of fear that frightened the animal, who had never known the man to speak in such a way before. Something was the matter, and its suspicious nature sensed danger – it knew not what danger, but somewhere, somehow, in its brain arose an apprehension of the man. It flattened its ears down at the sound of the man's voice, and its restless, hunching movements and the liftings and shifting of its forefeet became more pronounced; but it would not come to the man. He got on his hands and knees and crawled towards the dog. This unusual posture again excited suspicion, and the animal sidled mincingly away.

The man sat up in the snow for a moment and struggled for calmness. Then he pulled on his mittens, by means of his teeth, and got upon his feet. He glanced down at first in order to assure himself that he was really standing up, for the absence of sensation in his feet left him unrelated to the earth. His erect position in itself started to drive the webs of suspicion from the dog's mind; and when he spoke peremptorily, with the sound of whip-lashes in his voice, the dog rendered its customary allegiance and came to him. As it came within reaching distance, the man lost his control. His arms flashed out to the dog and he experienced genuine surprise when he discovered that his hands could not clutch, that there was neither bend nor feeling in the fingers. He had forgotten for the moment that they were frozen and that they were freezing more and more. All this happened quickly, and before the animal could get away, he encircled its body with his arms. He sat down in the snow, and in this fashion held the dog, while it snarled and whined and struggled.

But it was all he could do, hold its body encircled in his arms and sit there. He realized that he could not kill the dog. There was no way to do it. With his helpless hands he could neither draw nor hold his sheath-knife nor throttle the animal. He released it, and it plunged wildly away, with tail between its legs, and still snarling. It halted forty feet away and surveyed him curiously, with ears sharply pricked forward. The man looked down at his hands in order to locate them, and found them hanging on the ends of his arms. It struck him as curious that one should have to use his eyes in order to find out where his hands were. He began threshing his arms back and forth, beating the mittened hands against his sides. He did this for five minutes, violently, and his heart pumped enough blood up to the surface to put a stop to his shivering. But no sensation was aroused in the hands. He had an impression that they hung like weights on the ends of his arms, but when he tried to run the impression down, he could not find it.

A certain fear of death, dull and oppressive, came to him. This fear quickly became poignant as he realized that it was no longer a mere matter of freezing his fingers and toes, or of his losing hands and feet, but that it was a matter of life and death with the chances against him. This threw him into a panic, and he turned and ran up the creek-bed along the old, dim trail. The dog joined in behind and kept up with him. He ran blindly, without intention, in fear such as he had never known in his life. Slowly, as he ploughed and floundered through the snow, he began to see things again – the banks of the creek, the old timber-jams, the leafless aspens, and the sky. The running made him feel better. He did not shiver. Maybe, if he ran on, his feet would thaw out; and, anyway, if he ran far enough, he would reach camp and the boys. Without doubt he would lose some fingers and toes and some of his face; but the boys would take care of him, and save the rest of him when he got there. And at the same time there was another thought in his mind that said he would never get to the camp and the boys; that it was too many miles away, that the freezing had too great a start on him, and that he would soon be stiff and dead. This thought he kept in the background and refused to consider. Sometimes it pushed itself forward and demanded to be heard, but he thrust it back and strove to think of other things.

It struck him as curious that he could run at all on feet so frozen that he could not feel them when they struck the earth and took the weight of his body. He seemed to himself to skim along above the surface and to have no connection with the earth. Somewhere he had once seen a winged Mercury, and he wondered if Mercury felt as he felt when skimming over the earth.

His theory of running until he reached camp and the boys had one flaw in it; he lacked the endurance. Several times he stumbled, and finally he tottered, crumpled up, and fell. When he tried to rise, he failed. He must sit and rest, he decided, and next time he would merely walk and keep on going. As he sat and regained his breath, he noted that he was feeling quite warm and comfortable. He was not shivering, and it even seemed that a warm glow had come to his chest and trunk. And yet, when he touched his nose or cheeks, there was no sensation. Running would not thaw them out. Nor would it thaw out his hands and feet. Then the thought came to him that the frozen portions of his body must be extending. He tried to keep this thought down, to forget it, to think of something else; he was aware of the panicky feeling that it caused, and he was afraid of the panic. But the thought asserted itself, and persisted, until it produced a vision of his body totally frozen. This was too much, and he made another wild run along the trail. Once he slowed down to a walk, but the thought of the freezing extending itself made him run again.

And all the time the dog ran with him, at his heels. When he fell down a second time, it curled its tail over its forefeet and sat in front of him, facing him, curiously eager and intent. The warmth and security of the animal angered him, and he cursed it till it flattened down its ears appeasingly. This time the shivering came more quickly upon the man. He was losing in his battle with the frost. It was creeping into his body from all sides. The thought of it drove him on, but he ran no more than a hundred feet, when he staggered and pitched headlong. It was his last panic. When he had recovered his breath and control, he sat up and entertained in his mind the conception of meeting death with dignity. However, the conception did not come to him in such terms. His idea of it was that he had been making a fool of himself, running around like a chicken with its head cut off – such was the simile that occurred to him. Well, he was bound to freeze anyway, and he might as well take it decently. With this newfound peace of mind came the first glimmerings of drowsiness. A good idea, he thought, to sleep off to death. It was like taking an anaesthetic. Freezing was not so bad as people thought. There were lots worse ways to die.

He pictured the boys finding his body next day. Suddenly he found himself with them, coming along the trail and looking for himself. And, still with them, he came around a turn in the trail and found himself lying in the snow. He did not belong with himself any more, for even then he was out of himself, standing with the boys and looking at himself in the snow. It certainly was cold, was his thought. When he got back to the States he could tell the folks what real cold was. He drifted on from this to a vision of the old-timer on Sulphur Creek. He could see him quite clearly, warm and comfortable, and smoking a pipe.

'You were right, old hoss; you were right,' the man mumbled to the old-timer of Sulphur Creek.

Then the man drowsed off into what seemed to him the most comfortable and satisfying sleep he had ever known. The dog sat facing him and waiting. The brief day drew to a close in a long, slow twilight. There were no signs of a fire to be made, and, besides, never in the dog's experience had it known a man to sit like that in the snow and make no fire. As the twilight drew on, its eager yearning for the fire mastered it, and with a great lifting and shifting of forefeet, it whined softly, then flattened its ears down in anticipation of being chidden by the man. But the man remained silent. Later, the dog whined loudly. And still later it crept close to the man and caught the scent of death. This made the animal bristle and back away. A little longer it delayed, howling under the stars that leaped and danced and shone brightly in the cold sky. Then it turned and trotted up the trail in the direction of the camp it knew, where were the other food-providers and fire-providers.

A Vendetta
Guy de Maupassant

Paolo Saverini's widow lived alone with her son in a tiny cottage on the ramparts of Bonifacio. The town, built on a mountain spur, in some places actually overhanging the sea, faces the low-lying coast of Sardinia across the strait with its bristling reefs. At its foot on the other side it is almost entirely enclosed by a gash in the cliff like a gigantic passage, which serves as its harbour. The little Italian or Sardinian fishing-boats and once a fortnight the old puffing steamer, which runs to and from Ajaccio, come up as far as the first houses, after threading their way between two **precipitous** walls of rock.

On the white mountain-side the collection of houses makes a whiter patch. They look like the nests of wild birds clinging to the rock looking down on this dangerous channel, into which few ships venture. The wind harasses the sea remorselessly, sweeping the barren coast sparsely covered with coarse grass; it roars down the strait, stripping the land bare on both sides. Patches of whitish foam round the black tips of the countless reefs, which pierce the waves in every direction, look like torn sheets floating and drifting on the surface of the water.

The widow Saverini's house, clinging to the very edge of the cliff, had three windows opening on to this wide desolate view.

She lived there alone with her son, Antoine, and their dog, Frisky, a great raw-boned bitch, with a long, rough coat, of the sheep-dog breed. The young man used her as a gun-dog. One evening, after a quarrel, Antoine Saverini was treacherously

---

precipitous high and steep

knifed by Nicolas Ravolati, who escaped to Sardinia the same night.

When the old woman received her son's body, brought to her house by the passers-by, she shed no tears, but stood motionless for a long while, gazing at it; then, stretching out her wrinkled hand over the corpse, she vowed vengeance. She refused to let anyone stay with her, and shut herself up with the body and the howling dog.

The animal never stopped howling, standing at the foot of the bed, with head stretched out towards her master and tail between her legs. She stood as still as the mother, who bent over the body with staring eyes, now weeping silently, as she looked at him.

The young man, lying on his back, wearing his home-spun tweed jacket, with holes and rents in the breast, seemed to be asleep; but there was blood everywhere – on his shirt, which had been torn for first-aid dressings, on his waistcoat, on his trousers, on his face and on his hands. There were clots of dried blood on his beard and hair.

His aged mother began to speak to him; at the sound of her voice the dog stopped howling.

'Don't worry, my boy, my poor child, I will avenge you. Do you hear me? It's your mother's promise, and your mother always keeps her word, you know that.'

And slowly she bent over him, pressing her cold lips against the dead man's lips. Then Frisky began howling again, uttering a long, drawn-out moan, monotonous, piercing, sinister.

They stayed there, the two of them, the woman and the dog, till morning.

Antoine Saverini was buried next day, and he was soon forgotten in Bonifacio.

He had left neither brother nor near relative, so there was no one to take up the vendetta on his behalf.

His old mother was the only person who never forgot.

Across the strait all day long she could see a white speck on the coast. It was the little Sardinian village of Longosardo, where Corsican bandits took refuge when hard pressed by the police. They were almost the only inhabitants of the hamlet, facing the coast of their own country, and they waited there till it was safe to come back and return to the '**maquis**'. It was in this village, she knew, that Nicolas Ravolati had taken refuge.

Entirely alone she sat all day long at her window and gazed at this village, dreaming of her vengeance. How was she to carry it out? She was a weak woman, with not much longer to live, but she had promised it, she had sworn it on the body. She could not forget or put it off. What was she to do? Now she could not sleep at night; she had no rest, no peace of mind, obstinately determined to find a way.

The dog dozed at her feet and at intervals raised her head and howled into space. Since her master's death, she often howled in this way, as if calling him; she would not be comforted, as if her animal soul also carried an **indelible** memory.

One night, as Frisky began to howl, the mother had a sudden inspiration, the fierce **vindictive** inspiration of a savage. She pondered over it all night, and, getting up at daybreak, she went to the church. There she prayed, bowed down on the stone floor, humbling herself before God, seeking help and support, praying that her poor worn out body might have the strength to avenge her son.

Then she went home. She had in her back yard an old stove-in barrel, which collected the rain-water from the gutters; she turned it upside down, emptied it and fixed it on the ground

---

maquis the scrubby vegetation in Corsica where the bandits would hide out
indelible impossible to remove
vindictive desiring revenge

with stakes and stones; next she chained Frisky in this kennel and went into the house.

That day she spent hours walking up and down restlessly in her room, her gaze always fixed on the coast of Sardinia, the refuge of the assassin.

The dog howled all day and all night. In the morning the old woman took her a bowl of water, but nothing else – no bread or soup.

Another day passed. Frisky slept, weak with hunger. Next day her eyes were shining, her coat bristling and she was tugging furiously at the chain.

Still the old woman gave her no food. The animal, by now maddened with hunger, kept up her hoarse barking. Another night passed. At dawn the widow Saverini went to a neighbour's house and begged two trusses of straw. She took some of her late husband's clothes and stuffed them with the straw to resemble a human body.

Having fixed a stake in the ground in front of Frisky's kennel, she fastened the dummy to it, so that it looked like a man standing there, and made a head out of a roll of old linen.

The dog looked at the straw man in surprise, and stopped howling, in spite of her hunger.

Next the old woman went to the pork-butcher's and bought a long piece of black blood-sausage. Returning home, she lit a wood fire in the yard near the kennel and grilled the sausage. Frisky, maddened, leapt about and foamed at the mouth, her eyes fixed on the grilling meat, the smell of which sharpened her appetite.

At last the old woman made this steaming savoury mess into a scarf round the dummy's neck. She tied it there with string, leaving it for some time, so that it soaked well into the straw. This done, she untied the dog.

With one terrific bound the animal leapt at the dummy's throat, and with her paws on the shoulders began to tear at it. She dropped to the ground with some of the meat in her mouth; then she returned to the attack, burying her teeth in the string, and tore out more bits of sausage, dropped once more to the ground, and again attacked with mad fury. She tore the face to pieces and reduced the whole throat to ribbons.

The old woman, motionless and silent, watched the dog with tense excitement. Then she chained her up again, kept her without food for another two days and repeated the strange performance.

For three months she trained the dog to this kind of fight, making her use her teeth to get her food. Now she no longer chained her up, but set her on the dummy with a gesture.

She had taught her to go for the figure and tear it to pieces, even when there was no food hidden in the neck. Afterwards she rewarded the animal with the sausage she had grilled for her.

Whenever the dog saw the dummy, she immediately quivered all over, and looked towards her mistress, who cried in a shrill voice, pointing: 'At him!'

When she thought the time had come, she went to Confession and received the Sacrament one Sunday morning with **ecstatic fervour**; then, dressing in man's clothes to look like an old ragged beggar, she struck a bargain with a Sardinian fisherman, who took her, together with the dog, across the strait.

She carried a big piece of sausage in a canvas bag. Frisky had had nothing to eat for two days. The old woman kept making her smell the savoury food to excite her.

They reached Longosardo, and the old Corsican woman hobbled along to the baker's and enquired for Nicolas Ravolati's

---

ecstatic fervour a joyful, intense feeling

house. He had resumed his old trade as a joiner, and was working alone at the back of his shop.

The old woman pushed open the door and shouted: 'Hullo! Nicolas!' He turned round; then, slipping the dog's lead, she cried: 'At him! Go for him, tear him to pieces!'

The starving animal leapt at him and seized his throat. The man, throwing out his arms, grappled with the dog and fell to the ground. For a few seconds he writhed, kicking the ground with his heels. Then he lay still, while Frisky wrenched at his throat, tearing it to ribbons. Two neighbours, sitting at their doors, remembered distinctly seeing an old beggar come out of the shop with an emaciated black dog; as it walked, it was eating something brown, which its master gave it.

The old woman returned home in the evening. That night she slept soundly.

The Ugly Wife
Anthony Horowitz

This is a tale of King Arthur, the legendary king of Britain who ruled over the famous Knights of the Round Table. It is also about Sir Gawain, the nephew of King Arthur and the noblest of those who sat at the Round Table. It begins (as so many of these tales do) with a damsel in distress.

She came while the court was in Carlisle. Her hair was bedraggled, her clothes torn and her eyes wild with grief.

'Help me, King Arthur!' she cried. 'My husband has been stolen from me and enslaved by the wicked knight of Tarn Wathelyne. Though I fought him – see how my clothes are torn – there was nothing I could do. My husband is gone! And so I turn to you, great king. Give him back to me. Slay the knight of Tarn Wathelyne.'

When King Arthur heard this, he was shocked but pleased at the same time. The sight of the poor woman genuinely moved him, of course, but he secretly loved adventure and couldn't help looking forward to this new challenge. The very same day he set out on his horse. He went alone, armed only with a spear and with Excalibur, his magic sword, and as he went he whistled. For King Arthur had never known fear – or if he had, he had never shown it.

But this time something very strange happened. As he rode further and further into a wood (which became steadily darker and darker), the whistle died on his lips. He passed a lake as black as blood on a moonless night and his whole body shivered. All the trees had lost their leaves. Their branches writhed like snakes in the wind and ragged crows hung above them, laughing in the horrible way that crows do. King Arthur's teeth began to chatter. At last he saw the knight's castle. It was vast, wider at the top than at the bottom, with two dark windows high up and a solid black portcullis below. From a distance you could have mistaken it for an enormous human skull. It was as much as King Arthur could do to point his horse towards the drawbridge. But when the portcullis opened with a loud metallic creaking and the knight of Tarn Wathelyne rode out, the last of his courage left him. With a groan, he fell to the ground, almost fainting with fear.

The knight, invisible in his black armour, dismounted from his horse and walked over to where Arthur knelt. The king could not find the strength to look up. He heard the crunch of footsteps on gravel and the clink of armour. Then came the sound of metal scraping against metal as the knight drew out his sword. There was a minute's silence that seemed to drag on for an hour. Finally came a voice as cold as death itself.

'So this is the great King Arthur!' it whispered. 'Tell me – king – why should I not lop off your head while you grovel before me?'

'You … are … the … devil!' King Arthur gasped.

'No!' The knight laughed. 'My name is Gromer Somer Joure and I am the servant of Queen Morgan le Fay, your sworn enemy. But see – the lady is here, with me.'

With an effort, King Arthur raised his head and there standing beside the knight was the woman who had sent him on the quest in the first place. But now she was smiling **malevolently** at him. Morgan had magically disguised herself and even in his fear, King Arthur trembled with anger at how easily he had been deceived.

'Have pity on me!' he cried.

---

malevolently with evil intent

'Killing you now would be too easy,' the knight replied. 'So instead I will send you on a quest. Swear to me that you will return here, on your own, exactly one year from now. But when you come back, you must answer me this question. What is it that women want most in the world? If you can give me the correct answer, I will spare your miserable life. But if you are wrong, then, King Arthur, you will die. You will die slowly – and your bones will decorate my castle walls.'

The knight laughed. The lady laughed. Then they moved away. The portcullis came crashing down and King Arthur was left alone.

The Answer

'It was sorcery, my lord,' Gawain cried when he heard this story. 'It was black magic. That was what caused your fear. That is what made you cry for pity. By your leave, I will ride out to the castle and...'

'No, my dear Gawain,' King Arthur stopped him. 'I have been sent on a quest. I am honour-bound. What is it that women most desire in this world? I have a year to find out.'

'Then I will come with you,' Gawain said. 'Maybe together we'll have more luck.'

So together they left Carlisle and rode out across the country, stopping every woman they met in an attempt to find the answer to the knight's question. But they soon found themselves with more answers than they knew what to do with. Some said that women most desired jewels and fine clothes, others said a good husband and loving children. Luxury, loyalty, immortality, independence ... these were just some of the answers they received. There was one old lunatic who insisted that all women really wanted was strawberry jam. The answers ranged from the bizarre to the banal – but not one of them seemed entirely convincing.

Time passed quickly. A week turned into a month. Another month passed, then two, then six… Soon King Arthur and Sir Gawain found themselves on the way back to the enchanted castle. They had a whole catalogue of answers in their saddlebags, but both knew in their hearts that they had failed.

It was on the day before they were to part company, perhaps for ever, that they met an old woman. They had stopped in a clearing to rest their horses when Gawain saw her, sitting beside a stream, reading a book. His first thought was that she was beautifully dressed, for she wore the finest materials and her whole body was covered with jewels. Then she turned her head and he realised that she was without doubt the ugliest woman he had ever seen.

She really was incredibly ugly. Her two lips, like those of a chimpanzee, met several inches in front of her nose and when she smiled (and seeing Gawain, she did indeed smile), her teeth stuck out, yellow and uneven. Her skin was the colour and the texture of rice pudding and her hair would have looked better on a camel. Her nose had been pushed into her face until it had almost disappeared and she had such a bad squint that she seemed to be trying to look up her own nostrils. Finally, she was horrendously fat – so fat, in fact, that her hands and feet appeared to sprout out of her body without the benefit of arms and legs.

But she was a woman and, seeing her, King Arthur decided to have one last crack at the question. He approached her, bowing courteously, but before he could speak, she addressed him in a weird, cackling voice.

'I know the question you wish to ask,' she screeched, 'and I also know the answer. But I will give it to you on one condition only.'

'And what is that?' King Arthur demanded.

The horrible woman grinned at Gawain and ran a wet tongue over her lips.

'That knight...' she said, giggling. 'He is young and handsome. What lovely fair hair! What delicate blue eyes! I rather think I fancy having him as my husband. That is my condition! If you will give him to me in marriage, I will save your life.'

At this, Gawain went pale. He was indeed young and good-looking. All his friends expected him to come home one day with a beautiful wife. What would they say if he was coupled with this monster...?

But even as these thoughts rushed into his mind, second, nobler thoughts prevailed. He had a duty – to his uncle, and to the king.

'My lord,' he said. 'If this woman can save your life...'

'I can! I can!' the ugly woman crooned.

'...then gladly will I marry her.'

'My dear nephew,' King Arthur cried, 'I couldn't let you do that.'

'You cannot stop me,' Gawain replied. He fell onto one knee. 'Lady,' he exclaimed. 'I pledge you my word as a Knight of the Round Table that I will marry you if you can save the king. Tell him what it is that women most desire – and what you desire you will have.'

And so it was that the next morning King Arthur rode – alone as he had promised – to the castle of Tarn Wathelyne. Once again the sense of evil surrounded him like a great darkness, but this time he was able to ride forward with confidence, as though the answer he carried was a blazing beacon. For a second time the great portcullis ground open and the black knight rode out, his sword already unsheathed.

'Well – King?' he growled. 'Tell me the answer to my question. What is it that women most desire in this world?'

King Arthur replied boldly and clearly, repeating what the ugly woman had said to him. 'It is this,' he said, 'that they should have their will and that they should rule over men.'

For a moment the black knight was silent. Then he dropped his sword and, to Arthur's astonishment, fell to his knees.

'You have answered correctly, sire,' he said, 'and by doing so you have broken the spell which that evil witch Morgan le Fay had cast over me. She forced me to send you on your quest. I was her unwilling slave. But now her magic is ended, I beg you, sire, let me come and serve you at the Round Table. For beneath this foul black armour I am a good man and will prove myself worthy of you.'

'You are welcome,' King Arthur said, and as he spoke the dread castle of Tarn Wathelyne cracked and crumbled and suddenly there was a rushing wind as the bricks and ironwork shimmered in the darkness. Then the sunlight broke through the clouds. The castle shattered, the ground beneath it heaving as if glad to be finally rid of it. A moment later it had vanished, and once again the birds were singing.

'Let us ride together,' King Arthur said, and together they turned back to the court. But although the adventure had ended well for him, his heart was heavy. He had a wedding to attend, a nephew to see married. He would have given his kingdom for it to be otherwise.

The Wedding

The marriage of Sir Gawain was an event that nobody would ever forget. The ugly woman giggled during the service and ate so grotesquely at the feast afterwards that almost as much food went down her dress as into her mouth. She called King Arthur 'Warty' and forgot everyone's names. Of course, this being the age of chivalry, everybody managed to be tremendously polite. When Sir Gawain's new wife got drunk and fell over, they rushed forward to help her up as if she had merely stumbled. When she made impossibly rude jokes, they laughed and applauded. And they all congratulated Sir Gawain on his good fortune with as much sincerity as they could muster.

Poor Gawain was the politest of all of them. Not once did he let on that he had married the ghastly woman because he had been forced to. He called her 'my lady' and held her arm on the way to the table. When she emptied (or knocked over) her wine goblet, he refilled it for her. And although he was rather more silent than he was wont to be, and although he was certainly somewhat pale, he continued to behave as though nothing was wrong.

But at the end of the evening, when he found himself alone in the bedchamber with his ugly wife and watched her powdering her nose and all three of her chins, it all proved too much for him. He clutched his sword. He clutched his hair. Then he burst into tears.

'What is it, my little plum?' the lady asked. 'What has so upset you on your wedding night?'

'Lady,' Gawain replied, 'I cannot conceal my thoughts from you. You forced me to be your husband. In truth, I would rather not.'

'And why not?' the lady demanded.

'I cannot say.'

'Tell me!'

'Very well.' Gawain took a deep breath. 'I do not want to offend you, my lady, but you are old, ugly and evidently of low birth. Forgive me. I speak only what I feel.'

'But what's so wrong?' the woman gurgled. 'With age come wisdom and discretion. Are these not good things for a wife to possess? Maybe I am ugly. But if so, you will never need fear rivals while you are married to me. Is this not a good thing? Finally, you accuse me of being of low birth. Are you really such a snob, Gawain? Do you think that nobility comes just because you are born into a good family? Surely it depends on the character of a person! Can you not teach me to be noble like you?'

Gawain thought for a moment. Despite his innermost feelings, he could not help but agree that the old woman had a point. At the same time, he felt ashamed. Whatever he thought of her, she had saved the life of his uncle. He had behaved badly towards her. He had not behaved like a Knight of the Round Table.

'My lady,' he said. 'You are right in everything you say. I have spoken discourteously towards you and I apologise.'

'Then come to bed,' she said. But even as she spoke, Gawain detected something different in her voice and when he turned round he saw to his amazement that she had changed. It was no fat and ugly woman who lay on his bed but a young, beautiful girl with fair skin and soft, brown eyes.

'Gawain,' she said, smiling at him. 'Let me explain. Gromer Somer Joure, or the black knight, as you knew him, is my brother. Both of us were enslaved by the wicked Queen Morgan le Fay. I helped the king to release my brother from her spell but only the kindness and understanding of a noble spirit could save me from my horrible enchantment. That is what you have given me, dear Gawain, and now, at last, you see me as I really am. I am your wife – if you will have me. But this time the choice is really yours.'

Gawain gazed at her, speechless. Then he took her hand in his own and held it close to his cheek.

The next morning the court was astounded to see what had happened and the king ordered a second wedding feast so that this time everyone could really enjoy themselves. Gawain and his lady lived happily together for many years and, although nobody ever told the story when either of them was present (for fear of embarrassing them), on many a winter's night the knights and their pages would gather round the crackling fire to hear once again the strange tale of the ugly wife.

The Knight's Tale
Geoffrey Chaucer, retold by
Geraldine McCaughrean

Below the smoking walls of Thebes, two thousand men grappled, sword to sword and hand to hand. The battle between the forces of King Creon and the troops of Duke Theseus was long, fierce and bloody. And when it was over – when Creon's army had been put to flight – the ground was carpeted with fallen knights.

Athenian soldiers, searching the battlefield for their own wounded companions, found two young knights lying side by side. But as they stepped across the two bodies, one stirred, groaned, and opened his eyes. 'Arcite! Cousin! Where are you?' he whispered.

His companion was not dead, either. Both were carried as prisoners to the tent of Duke Theseus. 'Take them to Athens, and lock them in the prison-tower of my palace,' said the Duke.

Despite the cold stones and hard floor of their tower-top prison, both Arcite and his cousin Palamon gradually recovered from their wounds. Their devoted friendship made the passing days, weeks and months bearable, though both grew dreadfully bored.

The narrow arrow slit, which let in the only sunlight they ever saw, overlooked the Duke's garden. Each day they would take it in turns to balance on a stool and gaze down at the flowers, and at the gardener pruning the rose-trees.

One day there was a new visitor to the garden. Palamon was balancing on the stool at the time, and his feet slipped and almost tipped it over. 'Oh Arcite!' he exclaimed. 'I never realized until this moment why I was born. Now I've seen her. She is the reason! Zeus! She can't be flesh and blood. She must be an angel!'

'Come down. It's my turn for the stool,' said Arcite, and he took Palamon's place.

Down in the garden, Duke Theseus' young sister-in-law, Emily, had come to gather flowers in a wicker basket. She sang as she picked them – and the flowers seemed to turn up their faces towards her, and to faint at the touch of her hand.

'Oh lady! I'll wear your favour until the day I die!' said Arcite breathlessly to himself.

Palamon pulled the stool away, and they both fell in a heap to the floor. 'What? Are you making fun of me, Arcite? It's serious! I'm in love with her!'

'You? You didn't even think she was human! It's I who love her.'

'You Judas! You cuckoo! Where are your vows of lifelong friendship now? The first chance you get, you stab me in the back. You ... you ...'

'Viper! You thieving magpie!'

This undignified scene was interrupted by the gaoler bringing in their one frugal meal of the day. 'What's this, puppies?' he said, setting down the tray. 'Is this cell getting too small for the two of you? Well, I've got news for whichever one of you is Sir Arcite. Sir Arcite has a friend in Athens, it would appear. And this friend has spoken to Duke Theseus, and won your freedom. You can leave tomorrow.'

Arcite stared. Palamon got to his feet. 'Cousin!' he said. 'In all our lives, we have never been parted! Is there no message for *me*, gaoler? Has no one asked for *my* freedom?'

'No. You stay. And you, Sir Arcite, must be out of this land by sunset tomorrow. On pain of death are you forbidden to return.'

'Leave the country? Leave Athens? But I don't *want* to go!' protested Arcite. 'You go instead of me, Palamon. If I'm banished from Athens, I'll never see *her* again!'

Perhaps he saw, or perhaps he imagined a smile playing on Palamon's lips. Anyway, the two cousins, who all life long had been inseparable, barely spoke during that last night in the tower.

Next week, Palamon was still a captive, balancing all day on the stool to watch for Emily. Far away, his cousin sat in his own house, the windows and doors all shut as if it were a prison – for he was pining for Emily.

'Which do you think was better off?' mused the Knight, thoughtlessly interrupting his own story. 'Was it the man in prison or the man in exile?'

'Lord love you, have you no spark of wit?' demanded the lady I recognised from the night before by the enormous size of her hat. 'If the boy in exile had one half a brain he'd disguise himself and go back to Athens. If all he can do is sit around and mope, he doesn't *deserve* the woman!'

'Well, well,' said the Knight, rather taken aback by the strength of her feelings. 'That's just what happened.'

Arcite grew a beard, dressed as an Athenian, and took work as a servant in the very house where Emily lived. The thought of seeing her again quite outweighed the threat of death if he was discovered inside Athens.

Every day he saw her. Every day he took orders from her lips. Every day he was able to reach out and touch the chair where she had sat, the glass from which she had drunk. He thought he would be happy for ever.

He was happy for just a week. Then the questions began to creep into his mind. 'What good is this? How is this better than being in prison? How can a 'servant' speak of love to the sister-in-law of Duke Theseus?' So he fell to brooding, to chewing his pillow at night, and cursing the hour he was born.

Just two hours after the gaoler forgot to lock the door of the prison tower, Palamon found himself free, creeping through the Athenian woods, his heart in his mouth, his life in the balance. 'Now's my only chance,' he thought. 'I'll find the lady Emily and ravish her away to my own country.'

A rustling of leaves sent him bolting like a rabbit into the bowl of a hollow tree. He squatted down low, despising his thumping heart, and despising his fate for bringing an honourable knight to such a pass.

The approaching footsteps halted beside the tree, and Palamon held his breath. Surely the Duke's men were not searching for him yet? Peeping through a knot-hole, he could see a man sitting dejectedly among the spreading roots, throwing pebbles at his own boots. 'What's the use?' he was muttering. 'I might just as well be rotting in prison with Palamon.'

'You asp! You wolf-in-sheep's clothing!' Palamon flung himself out of the tree and grabbed Arcite by his beard. 'What are you doing, sneaking back here to prowl round my Emily?'

'Don't you talk about my mistress and lady like that, you convict, you escaped prisoner!'

'I'm an honourable knight!' Palamon maintained, despite the hammer-blows Arcite was raining on his head. 'I love Emily far more than you do!'

'Heartsblood! Death's too good for you, you traitor to all things honourable!'

'Goat!'

'Skunk!'

'Rat!'

As they pranced, grunting through the trees, their arms locked fast round one another, a wolfhound came barking round their legs excitedly. There was another – and another – and another – until the clearing was awash with dogs. Into the mêlée burst a hunting party on horseback, and at its head Duke Theseus himself.

'Part those men and bring them here! One of them is Emily's serving-man. The other looks like one of Creon's men!'

'He is! He's an escaped convict!' Arcite shouted.

'And he's Arcite – banished on pain of death!' called Palamon. 'You see, cousin? I can play as dirty as you!'

Theseus laughed in disbelief. 'Is this the devoted twosome we took prisoner at Thebes? Bosom friends never to be parted? In the name of all that's friendly, what's this quarrel about?'

Arcite and Palamon wiped their muddy faces, and rubbed their bruised eyes. Then both together they said: 'HER!'

Emily had come riding into the clearing on a white mare. She wore a blue mantle, and even the hounds fell back whimpering at the sight of her.

Arcite sprang to one stirrup, Palamon to the other. 'Lady, your eye has scorched me like a burning-glass!'

'Emily! Your name is a millstone crushing my heart!'

'Sweetheart, if I were to live two hundred...'

'Enough!' roared Theseus. 'What is this competition of compliments? If you're going to compete, at least do it the man's way! Tomorrow I'm holding a joust. Both your lives are forfeit, but I shall spare the man who remains alive when the joust ends. Prepare yourselves – for tomorrow you fight in the lists!'

Not until sundown, when they were billetted in separate tents on the field of combat, did Palamon and Arcite stop quarrelling. Outside Arcite's tent, an armourer was sharpening a sword with a stone. It grated and screeched. A chill went through the knight, but he called to mind Emily's radiant face, and went happily to sleep. Outside Palamon's tent, a squire was sharpening his master's lance with a knife. The shavings fell on to the canopy and made shadows like a swarm of spiders. A chill went through Palamon, but he thought of Emily, and how pleased she would be by his chivalrous heroism, and he went to sleep contented.

The joust was a circus of colour. Knights **caparisoned** in mail, heraldic surcoats, and plumes fit for birds of paradise were brazed by the blaring of trumpets whose scarlet **oriflammes** were embroidered with silvery beasts. Blade by blade, the grass was turfed out in divots by the flying hoofs of horses. The pavilions flapped like Chinese kites. By midday, the ladies tripping back and forth to their seats had scarlet hems where their gowns had swept the field.

In the hottest part of the day, Arcite and Palamon found themselves at opposite ends of the jousting fence. Palamon's lance weighed heavy in the crook of his arm after so many months in prison. The squires blew a shrill fanfare. The horses rattled the bits between their teeth and pranced towards one another.

On the first pass, both lances missed their mark, and the two cousins passed shoulder to shoulder, grimacing into one another's face.

On the second pass, Palamon saw the point of Arcite's lance bearing squarely for his chest. He flung himself forward along his horse's neck, dropping his own lance. But the oncoming lance-tip tore through the back of his tunic, caught in his belt, and lifted him out of the saddle, pitching him to the ground. Arcite's lance was dragged from his grip, but he turned at the head of the lists and came galloping back down the field, swinging his mace.

---

caparisoned decked out
oriflammes banners

Its iron spikes bruised the air with each whistling circle the mace-head made on its chain stalk. Palamon, his head uncovered, fell to his knees, but he knew he could not escape the swinging iron. In the grass, his hands brushed the lance that had dragged him from his horse. His fingers closed round its haft, and he was lifting it to protect himself, when Arcite, stretching from his saddle to strike the mortal blow, rode straight on to its point.

His face cleared of all expression. His horse rode from under him, and he stood for a moment with the lance planted in his chest. The mace dropped from his hand, and he spread his fingers across the red of his surcoat. 'Cousin,' he said, then fell dead on his back, the lance rising like a mast out of his hull.

Palamon took off his gauntlets and crawled across the grass to Arcite's side. 'Friend,' he said, touching his cousin's cheek. 'What have we done?'

Then the crowds were upon him, praising, congratulating. Duke Theseus was there, and Emily too, though Palamon could not recognise her at first among the other women. They were all quite pretty...

Theseus began: 'Arcite, my boy...'

'Palamon. I'm Palamon.'

'Oh. Well, Palamon, my boy, let this be an end to all quarrelling. Your rival has died a glorious death in the name of chivalry. And you have fought bravely, too. Take Emily's hand: and forget every unhappiness. The wedding shall be tomorrow!'

Hanging back in the shadow of her brother-in-law, Emily said: 'Urgh, do I have to? His hair's awfully thin already, and I don't like his mouth.' She had a voice like the teeth of a comb clicking.

'Nonsense, Emily. He's a very chivalrous knight – even if he is a foreigner. Emily – Arcite: my blessing on you both!'

'Palamon. I'm Palamon,' said the chivalrous knight, while at his feet Arcite raised no argument, no argument whatsoever.

The Knight stopped speaking. The woman in the enormous hat (who I learned was a widow all the way from Bath) had been leaning out of her saddle to catch the Knight's words. She was rather deaf, I think. She continued leaning towards him, waiting for more. 'Well?' she demanded in a huge, West Country voice. 'Were they happy?'

The Knight shook himself. 'Yes, oh yes. They both lived happily ever after. Palamon woke to each day happier than the day before.' The Widow smiled and sat back into her saddle with a thump.

'I don't know if he would – under the circumstances,' I said.

'Under *these* circumstances,' said the Knight, waving a hand towards the listening pilgrims, 'we had to have a happy ending. Now who's next?'

'All the same,' said a pebble-headed **Reeve** snarlingly, 'it wasn't a whole heap of laughs, your story.'

The Knight freely admitted it. 'I'm afraid I couldn't think of a *funny* story, offhand.'

'Well I can,' said the Reeve. We seemed to be about to hear his story, whether we liked it or not.

Reeve magistrate

The Tinker's Curse
Joan Aiken

One winter evening an old tinker who travelled from village to village selling his wares came to an isolated farmhouse which stood on the shore of a wide water. There were no other buildings near, and no sound to be heard but the distant cries of sheep, grazing on the moors.

But a light shone in the window of the little house, which cheered the tinker, who was hungry, and weary from his day's wandering.

He unpacked and set out his tray of goods, played a few notes on his bagpipes, and sang his tinker's chant:

Buy my beads and bobbins
My laces, silks and ribbons
Threads and pins and buttons
None so good as mine!

Then he knocked hopefully at the door. Usually, in such a lonely spot, he might be sure of a seat by the fire, a drink and a good meal, and an evening spent in singing songs and telling all the news of the country he had passed through.

How could he know that the house belonged to a heartless and wicked couple, a robber and his wife, who, without the least scruple, knocked the tinker on the head, cut his throat, and stole his money and goods. His body they tied to a stone and sank in the loch, and, as they were not able to play on the pipes, they threw those into the water after the body. And the night air echoed to their greedy laughter as they reeled back to the house, drunkenly singing:

Good night, tinker!

Sleep ye noo!
We'll mind yer wares for ye
The whole night through!

They thought they had seen the last of the tinker, but they were very wrong. For his angry ghost rose up out of the loch and haunted them, playing his pipes and howling for vengeance, until they could bear the place no longer, but left the croft and wandered away, witless with fear. And, in the end, it is told that they perished miserably, in a distant land.

Time went by. Nobody would live in the empty house, for the ghost continued to haunt it. But in the end, many years later, a poor young couple chanced to come that way, seeking for work and a place to live. Nobody had told them the tale of the tinker's ghost. When they saw the empty house they were overjoyed, for the young wife was soon to have a baby, and here, they thought, was just the place for them to settle. Happily, they stabled their donkey in the shed and unpacked their pots and pans.

The husband sang, as he knocked together a table and stools from some bits of wood he found on the shore:

Oh, what fun, we're going to have a son
I'll teach him how to throw a ball, teach him how to run
Teach him how to tickle trout, in the bubbling water –

And his wife gaily answered him, as she spread out the bedding to air, and fetched drinking water from the brook:

John, my dearie, don't forget – we might have a daughter!

Then suddenly she gave a sharp cry, as she felt the baby stir within her, and she called to her husband:

Mercy on us, love, my pains have begun
Go and fetch the doctor – quick, John – run!

'I'll fetch a doctor, sweetheart, never fear,' said John, and he dropped his hammer and raced off towards the nearest village, three miles away down at the foot of the loch.

But while he was on his way, dusk fell, and the tinker's ghost came up out of the water, playing a wild and grieving tune on his pipes. And the ghost sang:

If any hear me
Who will not help me
On you I lay my bane
Who will not help me
May ill befall you
Woman, child, or man!

The young wife heard him, and she shuddered in terror. 'Ghost, ghost, what have I ever done to you that you should hurt me?'

But, taking no notice of her, the spectre sang:

If you hear me
And do not help me
If I cry in vain
Hear no sound
From this day forward,
Never hear again!

When the young husband and the doctor came panting back to the croft, they found that they had come too late. For the wife had given birth to her baby, but now lay dead and cold, killed by the tinker's curse. Only the baby lived, wailing with hunger in her mother's arms.

'Take comfort, at least, from the child,' said the doctor. 'It's a bonny lass – see her sweet face.'

But John fell into a rage.

A bonny lass?
My wife is gone?
I want no lass
I want a son!

And from that day on, John retired into a hard shell of anger and useless grief and disappointment. He never spoke to Helen, his little daughter, except to scold or curse her; though she grew up pretty as a wild-rose, and sweet-tempered, worked as hard as she could to please him, and never said a word to provoke him.

How could she? For she was deaf. Doomed by the tinker's curse, she had never heard a single sound since the moment of her birth. She could not hear the lark twitter, nor the lambs bleat; she could not hear the fox bark, nor the curlew call; she could not hear the wind in the rowans, nor the patter of rain on the roof. And (more luckily for her) she could not hear her father's angry voice, though she could see his furious face. She lived in a shell of silence, as he did in a shell of anger.

And, because Helen could hear nothing, she was not able to speak. For how can you learn to use words if you have never heard them?

The children from the village at the loch-foot used to tease Helen. Because she could not speak, they thought she was daft, simple-minded. They used to dance round her, singing:

Deafie, daftie, she can't hear
Creep up behind her and pull her hair
Deaf as an adder, deaf as a post
She was cursed by the tinker's ghost –
Let's see who can get up closest!

But Helen's father became even angrier if he found them teasing her. Not because he cared about the teasing, but because they kept her from her work – sweeping, cooking, tending the garden, feeding the fowls. He would chase the children away from his door, hurling stones after them, and furious words:

'Away wi' ye, scoundrelly weans! Let the useless girl at least get on with her sweeping.'

Helen used to watch the other children wistfully, longing to be allowed to join in their games when they played Red Rover, or

Grandmother's Steps. But how could she ask? She had no words to tell what she wanted.

One thing Helen did have. And that, perhaps, had grown from the fact that, since she could not hear what they were saying, she watched other people so very, very closely. She almost seemed able to discover what was hidden in their minds, their memories. She was able to tell, if something had been lost, where it had been left. And this, to the other children, seemed mysterious, almost magical.

'Helen, Helen, I've lost my ribbon!' a girl would cry, pointing to her tangled locks, making gestures to convey the tying of a hair-ribbon.

Lost my ribbon, where can it be?
Lost my garter climbing a tree
Lost my skip-rope, lost my ball
Don't know where it can be at all!
Shot my arrow into the air
Fell to earth I don't know where
Lost my knife, I lost my pen
Where will I ever find it again?

And, almost every time one of the children had lost some treasure, Helen would be able to lead them to the place where it lay. So, gradually, because of this, the children began to be more friendly to Helen. And a boy called Andie, who was brighter than the rest, and kinder as well, began to teach Helen how to talk in sign-language; and then, putting his hands on either side of her face, helping her mouth to move, he showed her how to make sounds, how to speak words, and name the objects that were all around her.

I, you, he, she, it
Tree, sun, house, trouser, shirt
Arm, leg, hair, cheek, eye,

Grass, flower, dog, bird, sky!
Now do you begin to puzzle it out?
Now d'you start to see what it's all about?

And Helen would slowly answer, with a tongue that felt clumsy and stiff because for twelve years it had never done anything like this:

Yes – now I begin to see
Sun, house, trouser, tree
Yes, now I think I understand
Arm, leg, cheek, hand...

But, although she had now begun to talk a little, in a queer, croaking voice, Helen's father never spoke to her. Nor would she have heard him if he had. For she was still deaf. She could not hear thunder, or cuckoos, or the kettle boil, or the bull bellow.

One day, when Helen was about fourteen, a stranger came to the village. He was not really a stranger: he was the doctor who, all those years ago, had arrived too late to save Helen's mother. That failure had made him so sad that he had left the village and gone away to study medicine in a foreign land so that, in the end, he hoped, he might make up, by saving hundreds of lives, curing hundreds of sick people, for that one life he had not been able to save. Now the doctor was wise and famous, head of a great College of Medicine. He had come to visit his old mother.

When he saw Helen, fetching water from the loch, he asked, 'Tell me, who is that lassie?'

And the children told him, 'Ah, she's the deafie, she's the daftie.'

Deafie, daftie, she can't hear
Creep behind her and pull her hair
Deaf as an adder, deaf as a post
She was cursed by the tinker's ghost.

But Andie exclaimed:

You are unfair to the girl
She is not daft at all!
She can see further than most
She can find what is lost
Not only lost things can she find
She can read what is in your mind.

'Talk to her like this, on your hands,' Andie told the doctor. 'She can understand that very well.'

So, talking in sign language on his hands, the doctor asked Helen:

Can you really read my mind?
Do you know what I wish to find?

And Helen answered him directly:

You have lost your watch of gold
That tells both the time and the date
And has your name written inside the case

'How in the world did you know that, lassie?' exclaimed the doctor.

While you were fishing, up by the loch
The chain was loosened, the watch fell off
Up by the loch you'll find it safe
Under the shade of a foxglove leaf.

Helen led the doctor up to the loch and, sure enough, there was the watch lying, just where she had said it would be.

That watch was the gift of a grateful queen
Who was saved by my life-support machine!
I am overjoyed to have it found
I wouldn't have lost it for a thousand pound
What can I give you, Helen my dear?

And she answered:

Help me to hear! Help me to hear!

The doctor looked at her gravely. Then he said, 'Well; take me to your father.'

So she led the doctor to her father's house, and the doctor said to John: 'I would like to help your daughter.'

But John burst out, in his usual rage:

The girl's a fool, useless at her work
Deaf as a post, never hears a word
Never hear her laugh, never hear her sing
Never see her smile, never says a thing.

Fourteen years she has been my blight
Fourteen years next Saturday night
Ever since the curse of the tinker's ghost
When that brat was born and my love was lost.

'How deaf are you, Helen?' asked the doctor. 'Can you hear this?'

He took a tuning-fork from his bag, knocked it against the stone lintel, to make it hum, and held it, first in front of Helen's ear, then behind the ear, letting it touch the bone. After he had done many other tests, he told Helen and her father:

I could help this girl to hear
Two bones have joined inside her ear
With skill, with care
I could give her the power to hear.

John was not interested.

What good can it do?
You might make her worse
She is bound to be deaf
Because of the curse.

But the boy Andie cried:

Please help her, Doctor
With your clever knife
Open up her hearing

To all of life!

Helen herself wandered outside the cottage to think about what the doctor had said.

Do birds really sing?
Do boys really shout?
They open their mouths
But no sound comes out.

Do dogs really bark
Does the wind really blow?
Does the fire really crackle?
I don't know...

What is the sound
Of the sea on the shore
Does the bull bellow
Does the old man snore?

How can I tell
What is being said?
I have had to listen
To thoughts instead.

Then the doctor, coming out, warned her:

Attend now, Helen
Pay good heed
If I try this
It may not succeed.

Or, if you learn to hear
Then you may find
You have lost the power
To read my mind

You may lose the power
To find what's lost —

But Helen cried out:

Doctor, please do it
Whatever the cost!

And the children, gathering round, exclaimed:

What a surprise she's in for
When she first hears thunder
And won't she get a shock
When she first hears Rock!

Oh, but what a pleasure she has in store
To hear her first curlew, bubbling on the shore
– Yeah, but will she think it quite such fun
When she first hears somebody fire a gun?

The doctor took Helen away from the village to a grand hospital, far off in the city. And before he performed the operation on her ears, he warned her:

Helen, this is important
Please pay attention
After the operation
You must lie without moving a muscle
You must lie, still as a mummy
For a twenty-four-hour period
Your head flat, still on the pillow
No jerk, no twitch, no fidget.
Do you understand me?

'Yes,' said Helen. 'I understand.'

I must lie, without moving a muscle
For a twenty-four-hour period.

So Helen was put to sleep, and the doctor, with his tiny, delicate instruments, with wonderful skill and care, undid the two bones that were locked together inside her ear. And then she was wheeled back to her hospital bed, from the theatre where he had done the operation, and then she had to lie, still as a stone, for twenty-four hours. Not a muscle did she move. Her heart beat, her breath went in and out; that was all.

At the end of twenty-four hours, the doctor said to her,

'Helen, can you hear my voice?'

And she answered slowly, 'I am not sure.'

'I am going to put my gold watch beside your ear. Tell me if you can hear it tick.'

Helen listened, with her ear against the watch. She drew in a long, deep breath. Then she whispered:

Yes! It goes tick-tick-tick!
Tick – tick – tick – tick
Doctor, I never knew
What a wonderful sound a watch can make
Ticking the whole day through!

Tick, tick, tick, tick
Oh, what a beautiful sound
I could lie and listen for ever, for ever
Watching the hands go round!

When Helen went home to the village, the children came out to meet her, and cried,

Helen, can you hear?
Helen, can you hear us?
Did he open up your ears?
Can you hear our chorus?

And Helen told them:

Yes! I can hear, I can truly hear
All of a sudden, the whole world is near.
I can hear the trees rustle, hear the birds sing
I can hear the cuckoo, and the church bells ring
I hear the cricket chirping, and the plane overhead

I can hear the breadknife, cutting through the bread…

And they asked her,

Now your ears are open to sound
Can you hear our thoughts go round?
Do you still have that power of the other kind?
Can you still listen to another person's mind?

She told them:

No, I can hear your thoughts no longer
All I can hear is your speaking voice.
But this way round is really better
This way round is the safer choice.

Now I can hear your speaking voices
Nothing is gained without some cost
Now I can hear your thoughts no longer
Nor tell you where are the things you lost.

When he found that she was cured, that she was now like everybody else, Helen's father was sorry indeed that he had been unkind to her for so long. He walked by the loch, and said to himself,

Now her ears are open to sound
I forget my grief that she wasn't a son
I have done her great harm, all through her growing
But now I will atone for the wrong that I have done.

And he grew so kind that Helen could hardly believe it was the same man who had been sulky and full of rage all through her growing up.

The night that Helen came home, it took her a long time to fall asleep. The sounds of night were so beautiful – the wind, the bleating of sheep, the call of owls, the squeaking of bats – that she lay awake listening. And then, all of a sudden, she heard another sound. It was not her father, for he was down at the village, celebrating with his neighbours.

It was the ghostly tinker, playing a sad wild chant on his ghostly pipes. And he sang:

If any hear me
Who will not help me
On you I lay my bane
Who will not help me
May ill befall you
Woman, child, or man!

Helen, hearing this strange voice, threw a plaid round her shoulders and ran out of the house. And there she saw the tinker's ghost, all dripping wet, in the mist at the water's edge.

She cried:

Who are you, you poor old man?
With your pipes, and your pack?
Why, you are all wet! Let me help you
Take that heavy load from your back!

How can I help you, poor old man
Who have travelled so far?
Will you not come into our house
And sit by our fire?

The ghost told her:

If you would help me, find my poor bones
Where they lie in the dark
Find my skeleton that drifts uneasy
Below the waters of the loch

Bring my bones to the Christian kirkyard
Sort them tidy and bury them there
Wrapped and decent in shroud and coffin
Bid the Minister say a prayer

Set up a stone that tells my story

Only that will give me peace
Only when my bones are buried
Only then can I lie at ease.

And Helen promised:

Yes, I will find them, yes, poor ghost.
And bury them safe from wind and weather
Raise a stone that tells the story
Of the poor tinker's brutal murder
Candle and prayer shall help and hush you
Now your curse need travel no further.

So, the very next day, the tinker's bones were found and raised from the bottom of the loch, and given proper burial. And from that time his ghost haunted the place no longer.

Andie said to Helen, some months later, 'Helen! Do you really not know what I'm thinking any longer? Or can ye not guess?'

And she answered him:

People's thoughts should be safe and private
I've lost the power of the other kind –
But tell me what your thought is, Andie
The secret plan you have tucked behind?

And he said teasingly:

By and by I'll be telling you, Helen
Just for the moment – never you mind!

The Star-Child
Oscar Wilde

Once upon a time two poor Woodcutters were making their way home through a great pine-forest. It was winter, and a night of bitter cold. The snow lay thick upon the ground, and upon the branches of the trees: the frost kept snapping the little twigs on either side of them, as they passed: and when they came to the Mountain-Torrent she was hanging motionless in air, for the Ice-King had kissed her.

So cold was it that even the animals and the birds did not know what to make of it.

'Ugh!' snarled the Wolf, as he limped through the brushwood with his tail between his legs, 'this is perfectly monstrous weather. Why doesn't the Government look to it?'

'Weet! weet! weet!' twittered the green Linnets, 'the old Earth is dead, and they have laid her out in her white shroud.'

'The Earth is going to be married, and this is her bridal dress,' whispered the Turtle-doves to each other. Their little pink feet were quite frost-bitten, but they felt that it was their duty to take a romantic view of the situation.

'Nonsense!' growled the Wolf. 'I tell you that it is all the fault of the Government, and if you don't believe me I shall eat you.' The Wolf had a thoroughly practical mind, and was never at a loss for a good argument.

'Well, for my own part,' said the Woodpecker, who was a born philosopher, 'I don't care an atomic theory for explanations. If a thing is so, it is so, and at present it is terribly cold.'

Terribly cold it certainly was. The little Squirrels, who lived inside the tall fir-tree, kept rubbing each other's noses to keep themselves warm, and the Rabbits curled themselves up in their holes, and did not venture even to look out of doors. The only people who seemed to enjoy it were the great horned Owls. Their feathers were quite stiff with **rime**, but they did not mind, and they rolled their large yellow eyes, and called out to each other across the forest, 'Tu-whit! Tu-whoo! Tu-whit! Tu-whoo! what delightful weather we are having!'

On and on went the two Woodcutters, blowing lustily upon their fingers, and stamping with their huge iron-shod boots upon the caked snow. Once they sank into a deep drift, and came out as white as millers are, when the stones are grinding; and once they slipped on the hard smooth ice where the marsh-water was frozen, and their faggots fell out of their bundles, and they had to pick them up and bind them together again; and once they thought that they had lost their way, and a great terror seized on them, for they knew that the Snow is cruel to those who sleep in her arms. But they put their trust in the good Saint Martin, who watches over all travellers, and retraced their steps, and went warily, and at last they reached the outskirts of the forest, and saw, far down in the valley beneath them, the lights of the village in which they dwelt.

So overjoyed were they at their deliverance that they laughed aloud, and the Earth seemed to them like a flower of silver, and the Moon like a flower of gold.

Yet, after that they had laughed they became sad, for they remembered their poverty, and one of them said to the other, 'Why did we make merry, seeing that life is for the rich, and not for such as we are? Better that we had died of cold in the forest, or that some wild beast had fallen upon us and slain us.'

'Truly,' answered his companion, 'much is given to some, and

---

rime frost

little is given to others. Injustice has parcelled out the world, nor is there equal division of aught save of sorrow.'

But as they were bewailing their misery to each other this strange thing happened. There fell from heaven a very bright and beautiful star. It slipped down the side of the sky, passing by the other stars in its course, and, as they watched it wondering, it seemed to them to sink behind a clump of willow-trees that stood hard by a little sheep-fold no more than a stone's throw away.

'Why! there is a crock of gold for whoever finds it,' they cried, and they set to and ran, so eager were they for the gold.

And one of them ran faster than his mate, and outstripped him, and forced his way through the willows, and came out on the other side, and lo! there was indeed a thing of gold lying on the white snow. So he hastened towards it, and stooping down placed his hands upon it, and it was a cloak of golden tissue, curiously wrought with stars, and wrapped in many folds. And he cried out to his comrade that he had found the treasure that had fallen from the sky, and when his comrade had come up, they sat them down in the snow, and loosened the folds of the cloak that they might divide the pieces of gold. But, alas! no gold was in it, nor silver, nor, indeed, treasure of any kind, but only a little child who was asleep.

And one of them said to the other: 'This is a bitter ending to our hope, nor have we any good fortune, for what doth a child profit to a man? Let us leave it here, and go our way, seeing that we are poor men, and have children of our own whose bread we may not give to another.'

But his companion answered him: 'Nay, but it were an evil thing to leave the child to perish here in the snow, and though I am as poor as thou art, and have many mouths to feed, and but little in the pot, yet will I bring it home with me, and my wife shall have care of it.'

So very tenderly he took up the child, and wrapped the cloak around it to shield it from the harsh cold, and made his way down the hill to the village, his comrade marvelling much at his foolishness and softness of heart.

And when they came to the village, his comrade said to him, 'Thou hast the child, therefore give me the cloak, for it is meet that we should share.'

But he answered him: 'Nay, for the cloak is neither mine nor thine, but the child's only,' and he bade him Godspeed, and went to his own house and knocked.

And when his wife opened the door and saw that her husband had returned safe to her, she put her arms round his neck and kissed him, and took from his back the bundle of faggots, and brushed the snow off his boots, and bade him come in.

But he said to her, 'I have found something in the forest, and I have brought it to thee to have care of it,' and he stirred not from the threshold.

'What is it?' she cried. 'Show it to me, for the house is bare, and we have need of many things.' And he drew the cloak back, and showed her the sleeping child.

'Alack, goodman!' she murmured, 'have we not children enough of our own, that thou must needs bring a changeling to sit by the hearth? And who knows if it will not bring us bad fortune? And how shall we tend it?' And she was wroth against him.

'Nay, but it is a Star-Child,' he answered; and he told her the strange manner of the finding of it.

But she would not be appeased, but mocked at him, and spoke angrily, and cried: 'Our children lack bread, and shall we feed the child of another? Who is there who careth for us? And who giveth us food?'

'Nay, but God careth for the sparrows even, and feedeth them,' he answered.

'Do not the sparrows die of hunger in the winter?' she asked. 'And is it not winter now?' And the man answered nothing, but stirred not from the threshold.

And a bitter wind from the forest came in through the open door, and made her tremble, and she shivered, and said to him: 'Wilt thou not close the door? There cometh a bitter wind into the house, and I am cold.'

'Into a house where a heart is hard cometh there not always a bitter wind?' he asked. And the woman answered him nothing, but crept closer to the fire.

And after a time she turned round and looked at him, and her eyes were full of tears. And he came in swiftly, and placed the child in her arms, and she kissed it, and laid it in a little bed where the youngest of their own children was lying. And on the morrow the Woodcutter took the curious cloak of gold and placed it in a great chest, and a chain of amber that was round the child's neck his wife took and set it in the chest also.

So the Star-Child was brought up with the children of the Woodcutter, and sat at the same board with them, and was their playmate. And every year he became more beautiful to look at, so that all those who dwelt in the village were filled with wonder, for, while they were swarthy and black-haired, he was white and delicate as sawn ivory, and his curls were like the rings of the daffodil. His lips, also, were like the petals of a red flower, and his eyes were like violets by a river of pure water, and his body like the narcissus of a field where the mower comes not.

Yet did his beauty work him evil. For he grew proud, and cruel, and selfish. The children of the Woodcutter, and the other children of the village, he despised, saying that they were of mean parentage, while he was noble, being sprung from a Star, and he made himself master over them, and called them his servants.

No pity had he for the poor, or for those who were blind or maimed or in any way afflicted, but would cast stones at them and drive them forth on to the highway, and bid them beg their bread elsewhere, so that none save the outlaws came twice to that village to ask for alms. Indeed, he was as one enamoured of beauty, and would mock at the weakly and ill-favoured, and make jest of them; and himself he loved, and in summer, when the winds were still, he would lie by the well in the priest's orchard and look down at the marvel of his own face, and laugh for the pleasure he had in his fairness.

Often did the Woodcutter and his wife chide him, and say: 'We did not deal with thee as thou dealest with those who are left desolate, and have none to succour them. Wherefore art thou so cruel to all who need pity?'

Often did the old priest send for him, and seek to teach him the love of living things, saying to him: 'The fly is thy brother. Do it no harm. The wild birds that roam through the forest have their freedom. Snare them not for thy pleasure. God made the blind-worm and the mole, and each has its place. Who art thou to bring pain into God's world? Even the cattle of the field praise Him.'

But the Star-Child heeded not their words, but would frown and flout, and go back to his companions, and lead them. And his companions followed him, for he was fair, and fleet of foot, and could dance, and pipe, and make music. And wherever the Star-Child led them they followed, and whatever the Star-Child bade them do, that did they. And when he pierced with a sharp reed the dim eyes of the mole, they laughed, and when he cast stones at the leper they laughed also. And in all things he ruled them, and they became hard of heart, even as he was.

Now there passed one day through the village a poor beggar-woman. Her garments were torn and ragged, and her feet were bleeding from the rough road on which she had travelled, and she was in very evil plight. And being weary she sat her down under a chestnut-tree to rest.

But when the Star-Child saw her, he said to his companions, 'See! There sitteth a foul beggar-woman under that fair and green-leaved tree. Come, let us drive her hence, for she is ugly and ill-favoured.'

So he came near and threw stones at her, and mocked her, and she looked at him with terror in her eyes, nor did she move her gaze from him. And when the Woodcutter, who was cleaving logs in a **haggard** hard by, saw what the Star-Child was doing, he ran up and rebuked him, and said to him: 'Surely thou art hard of heart and knowest not mercy, for what evil has this poor woman done to thee that thou should'st treat her in this wise?'

And the Star-Child grew red with anger, and stamped his foot upon the ground, and said, 'Who art thou to question me what I do? I am no son of thine to do thy bidding.'

'Thou speakest truly,' answered the Woodcutter, 'yet did I show thee pity when I found thee in the forest.'

And when the woman heard these words she gave a loud cry, and fell into a swoon. And the Woodcutter carried her to his own house, and his wife had care of her, and when she rose up from the swoon into which she had fallen, they set meat and drink before her, and bade her have comfort.

But she would neither eat nor drink, but said to the Woodcutter, 'Didst thou not say that the child was found in the forest? And was it not ten years from this day?'

And the Woodcutter answered, 'Yea, it was in the forest that I found him, and it is ten years from this day.'

---

haggard wood

'And what signs didst thou find with him?' she cried. 'Bare he not upon his neck a chain of amber? Was not round him a cloak of gold tissue broidered with stars?'

'Truly,' answered the Woodcutter, 'it was even as thou sayest.' And he took the cloak and the amber chain from the chest where they lay, and showed them to her.

And when she saw them she wept for joy, and said, 'He is my little son whom I lost in the forest. I pray thee send for him quickly, for in search of him have I wandered over the whole world.'

So the Woodcutter and his wife went out and called to the Star-Child, and said to him, 'Go into the house, and there shalt thou find thy mother, who is waiting for thee.'

So he ran in, filled with wonder and great gladness. But when he saw her who was waiting there, he laughed scornfully and said, 'Why, where is my mother? For I see none here but this vile beggar-woman.'

And the woman answered him, 'I am thy mother.'

'Thou art mad to say so,' cried the Star-Child angrily. 'I am no son of thine, for thou art a beggar, and ugly, and in rags. Therefore get thee hence, and let me see thy foul face no more.'

'Nay, but thou art indeed my little son, whom I bare in the forest,' she cried, and she fell on her knees, and held out her arms to him. 'The robbers stole thee from me, and left thee to die,' she murmured, 'but I recognized thee when I saw thee, and the signs also have I recognized, the cloak of golden tissue and the amber-chain. Therefore I pray thee come with me, for over the whole world have I wandered in search of thee. Come with me, my son, for I have need of thy love.'

But the Star-Child stirred not from his place, but shut the doors of his heart against her, nor was there any sound heard save the sound of the woman weeping for pain.

And at last he spoke to her, and his voice was hard and bitter. 'If in very truth thou art my mother,' he said, 'it had been better hadst thou stayed away, and not come here to bring me to shame, seeing that I thought I was the child of some Star, and not a beggar's child, as thou tellest me that I am. Therefore get thee hence, and let me see thee no more.'

'Alas! my son,' she cried, 'wilt thou not kiss me before I go? For I have suffered much to find thee.'

'Nay,' said the Star-Child, 'but thou art too foul to look at, and rather would I kiss the adder or the toad than thee.'

So the woman rose up, and went away into the forest weeping bitterly, and when the Star-Child saw that she had gone, he was glad, and ran back to his playmates that he might play with them.

But when they beheld him coming, they mocked him and said, 'Why, thou art as foul as the toad, and as loathsome as the adder. Get thee hence, for we will not suffer thee to play with us,' and they drave him out of the garden.

And the Star-Child frowned and said to himself, 'What is this that they say to me? I will go to the well of water and look into it, and it shall tell me of my beauty.'

So he went to the well of water and looked into it, and lo! his face was as the face of a toad, and his body was scaled like an adder. And he flung himself down on the grass and wept, and said to himself, 'Surely this has come upon me by reason of my sin. For I have denied my mother, and driven her away, and been proud, and cruel to her. Wherefore I will go and seek her through the whole world, nor will I rest till I have found her.'

And there came to him the little daughter of the Woodcutter, and she put her hand upon his shoulder and said, 'What doth it matter if thou hast lost thy comeliness? Stay with us, and I will not mock at thee.'

And he said to her, 'Nay, but I have been cruel to my mother, and as a punishment has this evil been sent to me. Wherefore I must go hence, and wander through the world till I find her, and she give me her forgiveness.'

So he ran away into the forest and called out to his mother to come to him, but there was no answer. All day long he called to her, and when the sun set he lay down to sleep on a bed of leaves, and the birds and the animals fled from him, as they remembered his cruelty, and he was alone save for the toad that watched him, and the slow adder that crawled past.

And in the morning he rose up, and plucked some bitter berries from the trees and ate them, and took his way through the great wood, weeping sorely. And of everything that he met he made enquiry if perchance they had seen his mother.

He said to the Mole, 'Thou canst go beneath the earth. Tell me, is my mother there?'

And the Mole answered, 'Thou hast blinded mine eyes. How should I know?'

He said to the Linnet, 'Thou canst fly over the tops of the tall trees, and canst see the whole world. Tell me, canst thou see my mother?'

And the Linnet answered, 'Thou hast clipt my wings for thy pleasure. How should I fly?'

And to the little Squirrel who lived in the fir-tree, and was lonely, he said, 'Where is my mother?'

And the Squirrel answered, 'Thou hast slain mine. Dost thou seek to slay thine also?'

And the Star-Child wept and bowed his head, and prayed forgiveness of God's things, and went on through the forest, seeking for the beggar-woman. And on the third day he came to the other side of the forest and went down into the plain.

And when he passed through the villages the children

mocked him, and threw stones at him, and the **carlots** would not suffer him even to sleep in the byres lest he might bring mildew on the stored corn, so foul was he to look at, and their hired men drave him away, and there was none who had pity on him. Nor could he hear anywhere of the beggar-woman who was his mother, though for the space of three years he wandered over the world, and often seemed to see her on the road in front of him, and would call to her, and run after her till the sharp flints made his feet to bleed. But overtake her he could not, and those who dwelt by the way did ever deny that they had seen her, or any like to her, and they made sport of his sorrow.

For the space of three years he wandered over the world, and in the world there was neither love nor loving-kindness nor charity for him, but it was even such a world as he had made for himself in the days of his great pride.

And one evening he came to the gate of a strong-walled city that stood by a river, and, weary and footsore though he was, he made to enter in. But the soldiers who stood on guard dropped their halberts across the entrance, and said roughly to him, 'What is thy business in the city?'

'I am seeking for my mother,' he answered, 'and I pray ye to suffer me to pass, for it may be that she is in this city.'

But they mocked at him, and one of them wagged a black beard, and set down his shield and cried, 'Of a truth, thy mother will not be merry when she sees thee, for thou art more ill-favoured than the toad of the marsh, or the adder that crawls in the fen. Get thee gone. Get thee gone. Thy mother dwells not in this city.'

---

carlots peasants

And another, who held a yellow banner in his hand, said to him, 'Who is thy mother, and wherefore art thou seeking for her?'

And he answered, 'My mother is a beggar even as I am, and I have treated her evilly, and I pray ye to suffer me to pass that she may give me her forgiveness, if it be that she tarrieth in this city.' But they would not, and pricked him with their spears.

And, as he turned away weeping, one whose armour was inlaid with gilt flowers, and on whose helmet couched a lion that had wings, came up and made enquiry of the soldiers who it was who had sought entrance. And they said to him, 'It is a beggar and the child of a beggar, and we have driven him away.'

'Nay,' he cried, laughing, 'but we will sell the foul thing for a slave, and his price shall be the price of a bowl of sweet wine.'

And an old and evil-visaged man who was passing by called out, and said, 'I will buy him for that price,' and, when he had paid the price, he took the Star-Child by the hand and led him into the city.

And after that they had gone through many streets they came to a little door that was set in a wall that was covered with a pomegranate tree. And the old man touched the door with a ring of graved jasper and it opened, and they went down five steps of brass into a garden filled with black poppies and green jars of burnt clay. And the old man took then from his turban a scarf of figured silk, and bound with it the eyes of the Star-Child, and drave him in front of him. And when the scarf was taken off his eyes, the Star-Child found himself in a dungeon, that was lit by a lantern of horn.

And the old man set before him some mouldy bread on a trencher and said, 'Eat,' and some brackish water in a cup and said, 'Drink,' and when he had eaten and drunk, the old man went out, locking the door behind him and fastening it with an iron chain.

And on the morrow the old man, who was indeed the subtlest of the magicians of Libya and had learned his art from one who dwelt in the tombs of the Nile, came in to him and frowned at him, and said, 'In a wood that is nigh to the gate of this city of Giaours there are three pieces of gold. One is of white gold, and another is of yellow gold, and the gold of the third one is red. To-day thou shalt bring me the piece of white gold, and if thou bringest it not back, I will beat thee with a hundred stripes. Get thee away quickly, and at sunset I will be waiting for thee at the door of the garden. See that thou bringest the white gold, or it shall go ill with thee, for thou art my slave, and I have bought thee for the price of a bowl of sweet wine.' And he bound the eyes of the Star-Child with the scarf of figured silk, and led him through the house, and through the garden of poppies, and up the five steps of brass. And having opened the little door with his ring he set him in the street.

And the Star-Child went out of the gate of the city, and came to the wood of which the Magician had spoken to him.

Now this wood was very fair to look at from without, and seemed full of singing birds and of sweet-scented flowers, and the Star-Child entered it gladly. Yet did its beauty profit him little, for wherever he went harsh briars and thorns shot up from the ground and encompassed him, and evil nettles stung him, and the thistle pierced him with her daggers, so that he was in sore distress. Nor could he anywhere find the piece of white gold of which the Magician had spoken, though he sought for it from morn to noon, and from noon to sunset. And at sunset he set his face towards home, weeping bitterly, for he knew what fate was in store for him.

But when he had reached the outskirts of the wood, he heard from a thicket a cry as of someone in pain. And forgetting his own sorrow he ran back to the place, and saw there a little Hare caught in a trap that some hunter had set for it.

And the Star-Child had pity on it, and released it, and said to it, 'I am myself but a slave, yet may I give thee thy freedom.'

And the Hare answered him, and said: 'Surely thou hast given me freedom, and what shall I give thee in return?'

And the Star-Child said to it, 'I am seeking for a piece of white gold, nor can I anywhere find it, and if I bring it not to my master he will beat me.'

'Come thou with me,' said the Hare, 'and I will lead thee to it, for I know where it is hidden, and for what purpose.'

So the Star-Child went with the Hare, and lo! in the cleft of a great oak-tree he saw the piece of white gold that he was seeking. And he was filled with joy, and seized it, and said to the Hare, 'The service that I did to thee thou hast rendered back again many times over and the kindness that I showed thee thou hast repaid a hundredfold.'

'Nay,' answered the Hare, 'but as thou dealt with me, so I did deal with thee,' and it ran away swiftly, and the Star-Child went towards the city.

Now at the gate of the city there was seated one who was a leper. Over his face hung a cowl of grey linen, and through the eyelets his eyes gleamed like red coals. And when he saw the Star-Child coming, he struck upon a wooden bowl, and clattered his bell, and called out to him, and said, 'Give me a piece of money, or I must die of hunger. For they have thrust me out of the city, and there is no one who has pity on me.'

'Alas!' cried the Star-Child, 'I have but one piece of money in my wallet, and if I bring it not to my master he will beat me, for I am his slave.'

But the leper entreated him, and prayed of him, till the Star-Child had pity, and gave him the piece of white gold.

And when he came to the Magician's house, the Magician opened to him, and brought him in, and said to him, 'Hast thou the piece of white gold?' And the Star-Child answered, 'I have it not.' So the Magician fell upon him, and beat him, and set before him an empty trencher, and said 'Eat,' and an empty cup, and said, 'Drink,' and flung him again into the dungeon.

And on the morrow the Magician came to him, and said, 'If to-day thou bringest me not the piece of yellow gold, I will surely keep thee as my slave, and give thee three hundred stripes.'

So the Star-Child went to the wood, and all day long he searched for the piece of yellow gold, but nowhere could he find it. And at sunset he sat him down and began to weep, and as he was weeping there came to him the little Hare that he had rescued from the trap.

And the Hare said to him, 'Why art thou weeping? And what dost thou seek in the wood?'

And the Star-Child answered, 'I am seeking for a piece of yellow gold that is hidden here, and if I find it not my master will beat me, and keep me as a slave.'

'Follow me,' cried the Hare, and it ran through the wood till it came to a pool of water. And at the bottom of the pool the piece of yellow gold was lying.

'How shall I thank thee?' said the Star-Child, 'for lo! this is the second time that you have succoured me.'

'Nay, but thou hadst pity on me first,' said the Hare, and it ran away swiftly.

And the Star-Child took the piece of yellow gold, and put it in his wallet, and hurried to the city. But the leper saw him coming, and ran to meet him, and knelt down and cried, 'Give me a piece of money or I shall die of hunger.'

And the Star-Child said to him, 'I have in my wallet but one piece of yellow gold, and if I bring it not to my master he will beat me and keep me as his slave.'

But the leper entreated him sore, so that the Star-Child had pity on him, and gave him the piece of yellow gold.

And when he came to the Magician's house, the Magician opened to him, and brought him in, and said to him, 'Hast thou the piece of yellow gold?' And the Star-Child said to him, 'I have it not.' So the Magician fell upon him, and beat him, and loaded him with chains, and cast him again into the dungeon.

And on the morrow the Magician came to him, and said, 'If to-day thou bringest me the piece of red gold I will set thee free, but if thou bringest it not I will surely slay thee.'

So the Star-Child went to the wood, and all day long he searched for the piece of red gold, but nowhere could he find it. And at evening he sat him down, and wept, and as he was weeping there came to him the little Hare.

And the Hare said to him, 'The piece of red gold that thou seekest is in the cavern that is behind thee. Therefore weep no more but be glad.'

'How shall I reward thee,' cried the Star-Child, 'for lo! this is the third time thou hast succoured me.'

'Nay, but thou hadst pity on me first,' said the Hare, and it ran away swiftly.

And the Star-Child entered the cavern, and in its farthest corner he found the piece of red gold. So he put it in his wallet, and hurried to the city. And the leper seeing him coming, stood in the centre of the road, and cried out, and said to him, 'Give me the piece of red money, or I must die,' and the Star-Child had pity on him again, and gave him the piece of red gold, saying, 'Thy need is greater than mine.' Yet was his heart heavy, for he knew what evil fate awaited him.

But lo! as he passed through the gate of the city, the guards bowed down and made obeisance to him, saying, 'How beautiful is our lord!' and a crowd of citizens followed him, and cried out, 'Surely there is none so beautiful in the whole world!' so that the Star-Child wept, and said to himself, 'They are mocking me, and making light of my misery.' And so large was the concourse of the people, that he lost the threads of his way, and found himself at last in a great square, in which there was a palace of a King.

And the gate of the palace opened, and the priests and the high officers of the city ran forth to meet him, and they abased themselves before him, and said, 'Thou art our lord for whom we have been waiting, and the son of our King.'

And the Star-Child answered them and said, 'I am no king's son, but the child of a poor beggar-woman. And how say ye that I am beautiful, for I know that I am evil to look at?'

Then he, whose armour was inlaid with gilt flowers, and on whose helmet couched a lion that had wings, held up a shield, and cried, 'How saith my lord that he is not beautiful?'

And the Star-Child looked, and lo! his face was even as it had been, and his comeliness had come back to him, and he saw that in his eyes which he had not seen there before.

And the priests and the high officers knelt down and said to him, 'it was prophesied of old that on this day should come he who was to rule over us. Therefore, let our lord take this crown and this sceptre, and be in his justice and mercy our King over us.'

But he said to them, 'I am not worthy, for I have denied the mother who bare me, nor may I rest till I have found her, and known her forgiveness. Therefore, let me go, for I must wander again over the world, and may not tarry here, though ye bring me the crown and the sceptre.' And as he spake he turned his face from them towards the street that led to the gate of the city, and lo! amongst the crowd that pressed round the soldiers, he saw the beggar-woman who was his mother, and at her side stood the leper, who had sat by the road.

And a cry of joy broke from his lips, and he ran over, and kneeling down he kissed the wounds on his mother's feet, and wet them with his tears. He bowed his head in the dust, and sobbing, as one whose heart might break, he said to her: 'Mother, I denied thee in the hour of my pride. Accept me in the hour of my humility. Mother, I gave thee hatred. Do thou give me love. Mother, I rejected thee. Receive thy child now.' But the beggar-woman answered him not a word.

And he reached out his hands, and clasped the white feet of the leper, and said to him: 'Thrice did I give thee of my mercy. Bid my mother speak to me once.' But the leper answered him not a word.

And he sobbed again, and said: 'Mother, my suffering is greater than I can bear. Give me thy forgiveness, and let me go back to the forest.' And the beggar-woman put her hand on his head, and said to him, 'Rise,' and the leper put his hand on his head, and said to him 'Rise,' also.

And he rose up from his feet, and looked at them, and lo! they were a King and a Queen.

And the Queen said to him, 'This is thy father whom thou hast succoured.'

And the King said, 'This is thy mother, whose feet thou hast washed with thy tears.'

And they fell on his neck and kissed him, and brought him into the palace, and clothed him in fair raiment, and set the crown upon his head, and the sceptre in his hand, and over the city that stood by the river he ruled, and was its lord. Much justice and mercy did he show to all, and the evil Magician he banished, and to the Woodcutter and his wife he sent many rich gifts, and to their children he gave high honour. Nor would he suffer any to be cruel to bird or beast, but taught love and loving-kindness and charity, and to the poor he gave bread, and to the naked he gave raiment, and there was peace and plenty in the land.

Yet ruled he not long, so great had been his suffering, and so bitter the fire of his testing, for after the space of three years he died. And he who came after him ruled evilly.

Activities

Additional support for teaching these book activities can be found at www.heinemann.co.uk/literature

The additional support resources contain:

- a full scheme of work: 32 medium-term lesson plans
- Student Sheets, Teacher's Notes and OHTs to accompany the lesson plans.

The Heart of Another
by Marcus Sedgwick

1 Look again at the title of this story. Why do you think the writer chose it? Write down as many different reasons as you can think of.

2 Look at the table below. It shows a four-part structure which can be applied to almost any story. Write four sentences summing up 'The Heart of Another' using this structure.

	Little Red Riding Hood	The Heart of Another
Setting: the story is set up	A girl is going to visit her grandma	
Conflict: there is a problem	She meets a wolf	
Climax: the problem reaches its peak	The wolf wants to eat her	
Resolution: the problem is sorted out	A woodcutter kills the wolf	

3 The writer gives a lot of clues that build up towards the ending of the story. For example, the narrator develops a taste for beer after her operation. What does this suggest? What other clues can you find?

4 What do you think is happening at the end of the story? Is John a murderer? Or has the narrator gone mad?

The Tell-Tale Heart
by Edgar Allan Poe

1   **a**   Re-read the first paragraph of the story. Write down one word that sums up your first impression of the story's narrator.

    b   Try to find three quotations that support your first impression. For each one, write a sentence or two explaining why you chose it.

2   The narrator tells us 'There came to my ears a low, dull, quick sound ... It was the beating of the man's heart.'

- Do you believe that he can hear this?
- Do you believe everything he says, or is he an *unreliable narrator*?
- Find three more quotations where you find the narrator unreliable.
- For each one, try to work out what the writer might be *inferring* about the narrator or the events in the story.

3   Write three paragraphs about the narrator of this story using the structure:

- point (what the narrator tells us)
- evidence (quotation)
- explanation (what the writer wants us to infer).

The Writing on the Wall
by Celia Rees

1 Re-read the two opening paragraphs of the story. Write down all the words used to describe the weather and location. Then write down all the words used to describe the house. What do you notice? Why do you think the writer has chosen to do this?

2 The writer describes the roof of the house like this: '...the twin roofs of the gables rising like great arching brows, frowning a warning...'

   a What do these words suggest about the 'look' of the house?

   b What effect does the *simile* have (comparing the gables to eyebrows)?

   c What effect does the *personification* have (describing the house as 'frowning', a word normally used to describe humans)?

3 Choose one of the following descriptions:

   • the house, pages 31–2
   • the mummified cat, page 35
   • upstairs, page 39
   • the final confrontation, pages 44–6

Which is the most effective word in the description? What effect did the writer want to have on the reader? Which other words have a similar effect? Are there any that have a different effect? Why has the writer used them?

The Ghost in the Bride's Chamber
by Charles Dickens

1   Working with a partner, write down all the key events in the story on strips of paper. Jumble them up and exchange them with another pair. Can they put them in the right order?

2   The old man tells his story to two other characters in the story. Why do you think the writer chose to use this technique of a 'story within a story'? Hint: how do we feel when we find out that the old man is the ghost of the man in the story?

3   Although this is a ghost story, it has the kinds of characters you might expect to find in other types of story: a hero, a heroine and a villain. Which characters are which? Find a quotation to show what each of them is like. How do you think the writer wants the reader to respond to these characters? Use a table like the one below to record your answers.

	Name of character	Quotation	How the writer wants the reader to respond
Hero			
Heroine			
Villain			

Chicken
by Mary Hoffman

1 The writer gives us a clue as to how the story will develop in the very first paragraph. Why does she do this?

2 The writer gives us lots of examples of the gang's very early life together: 'We all learnt to swim together...' Compare this with the events described in the story. What is the effect?

3 Look at pages 69–70 (from 'And so it continued...' to '...take on the Terminator.'). What is happening in this part of the story? What do you notice about the start of most of the paragraphs on these pages? Why has the writer done this?

4 Like most stories, 'Chicken' can be summed up in a four-part structure, as in the table below. What reaction do you think the writer wanted the reader to have at each stage?

	Chicken
Setting: the story is set up	Some boys are in a gang
Conflict: there is a problem	They start giving each other dares
Climax: the problem reaches its peak	The dares become dangerous
Resolution: the problem is sorted out	The dares stop. The boys are friends

5 Does the writer want the reader to learn something from this story? What is the moral of this story?

The Destructors
by Graham Greene

1   Do you agree with the lorry driver's comment at the end of the story: '...you got to admit it's funny.'? If so, why? If not, why not?

2   What are your feelings about the character of Mr Thomas at the end of the story? Find a quotation to help you explain your answer.

3   What are your feelings about the characters of the boys at the end of the story? Find a quotation to help you explain your answer.

4   Look over the story again and find any quotations that tell you about the character of 'T'. What response do you think the writer wants the reader to have to this character? Write your findings in a table like this:

Quotation	What it tells us	My response
'He never wasted a word even to tell his name'	Quiet, shy, not very good at getting on with people	
'I've got a better idea ... we'll destroy it.'		

5   Does this story have a moral? If so, what is it? If not, what is the purpose of this story?

Porkies

by Robert Swindells

1. What response do you think the writer wants from the reader of this story? Write down three features or details from the story to support your answer.

2. Look carefully at the character of Piggo. Re-read the story, making a note about him every time he appears in the story. For each of those notes, write down your response to the character. Use a table like the one below to record your answers.

When we're told that Piggo...	Our response is...
tells lies	

3. At the end of the story, the writer does not describe Piggo's friends' reaction. What do you think it might have been?

4. Why do you think the writer ended the story in this way?

5. Plan three new endings that the writer could have used for 'Porkies'. For each one, write a sentence explaining how you think it would affect the reader's response to the story and to Piggo's character.

Billy the Kid
by William Golding

1   Re-read pages 107–9 from 'At the end of the morning...' to '... THEY DON'T LIKE ME!'.

    a   How does the writer suggest that the boys are fighting a war against Billy?

    b   Make a note of every time the writer uses the sense of hearing to describe the scene. What do you notice? Why do you think the writer has done this?

2   What do you think Miss said to the class in her 'fifteen minutes' sermon'?

3   What has Billy learned by the end of the story that helped him to win the prize for improvement?

4   Why do you think the writer chose the name of this story? Try to think of three reasons why it is an effective title.

5   Write a short description of a fight. Try to use the same techniques that you noted in question 1.

The Cats
by Robert Westall

1   Re-read the narrator's description of the tabby cat at the
start of the story on page 112. Make a note of the vocabulary
used to describe the cat, dividing it into positive and negative
language. You could use a table like the one below to record
your answers.

Positive language	Negative language
Prime specimen	blotched

What do you notice? What effect does this have?

2   What do you think happened at the end of the story? Write
your explanation in two or three sentences. Then write down
any questions you have about the ending. Share them with a
partner. Can you help answer each other's questions?

3   Look through the story to find each time a cat appears. Can
you see any link between the narrator's relationship with her
husband and the appearance of the cats?

4   Write down the stereotypical qualities that we expect of dogs
and cats. For example, 'dogs are faithful, they bark and growl...'
'cats are independent and much quieter...' In what ways are
the narrator and her husband like a cat and a dog?

The Brazilian Cat
by Arthur Conan Doyle

1 Why do you think the writer chose a Brazilian cat as the murder weapon in this story? Find a quotation from the story to support your answer.

2 Why did Everard King try to kill the narrator?

3 What information at the end of the story helped you work this out? Try to find at least two pieces of information.

4 Why do you think the writer withheld this information until the last page?

5 What *kind* of information does the writer withhold?

6 The writer gives us at least two clues to the ending in the middle of the story. What are they?

To Build a Fire
by Jack London

1 Whose fault is it that the man in the story dies? Write a sentence or two explaining your point of view.

2 Pick any paragraph in the story and find any words to do with cold. What do you notice? Why do you think this is?

3 Jack London originally wrote a story called 'To Build a Fire' six years before he wrote the one you have just read. Read the opening and the ending of the original version:

The opening

For land travel or seafaring, the world over, a companion is usually considered desirable. In the Klondike, as Tom Vincent found out, such a companion is absolutely essential...

He had left Calumet Camp on the Yukon with a light pack on his back, to go up Paul Creek to the divide between it and Cherry Creek, where his party was prospecting and hunting moose.

The ending

...In a month's time he was able to be about on his feet, although the toes were destined always after that to be very sensitive to frost. But the scars on his hands he knows he will carry to the grave. And – 'Never travel alone!' he now lays down the precept of the North.

---

4 What differences do you notice between the two versions? Why do you think the writer changed his story in these ways?

A Vendetta
by Guy de Maupassant

1 Re-read the first two paragraphs of the story, looking at the details the writer gives to describe the setting. Make a list of the key descriptive words the writer uses. Think of one word that would sum up this vocabulary selection.

2 How does the description reflect the kind of community in which this story is set?

3 Identify a sentence in which the writer describes Antoine, and in that one sentence, underline and comment on one word that you think is particularly effective. Now do the same for Widow Saverini, her dog, and Nicolas Ravolati.

4 Compare the amount of information we are given about these four characters. Which is the most important character in the story? Which is the least important? What does this suggest about the writer's intention in this story?

5 Do you think Widow Saverini is justified in killing Nicolas Ravolati?

6 What do you think the writer would say if he were asked the same question? Write a sentence or two explaining your answer.

The Ugly Wife
by Antony Horowitz

1 Think about other folk tales you have read or heard. What do they have in common with this tale? Think about the characters, the things that happen during the story and the way it ends.

2 Look again at the story up to '...both knew in their hearts that they had failed' on page 187. Find examples of the writer's use of these descriptive techniques:

- the sense of sight
- the sense of hearing
- onomatopoeia
- a list
- repetition
- alliteration.

3 For each of the above techniques, write a sentence explaining the effect you think the writer wanted to create.

Make a display poster headed 'Language techniques', showing the six descriptive techniques. For each one, give:

- a definition
- an example from 'The Ugly Wife'
- a comment on its effect.

Try to use presentation, e.g. symbols, pictures, different fonts, to reflect the meaning of the writer's, and your own, words.

The Knight's Tale
by Geoffrey Chaucer

1   Make a list of all the events in the story: what the characters do and what happens to them. For each one, write down the result of the event and what the writer is suggesting. Use a table like this:

Event	The result is...	The writer is suggesting that...
Palamon and Arcite see Emily.	They instantly fall in love	
Arcite is pardoned and freed.		

2   In Chaucer's version, Palamon and Emily are happy to marry each other – though a little sad at the death of Arcite. What differences does this suggest between Chaucer's and McCaughrean's viewpoints?

3   How would you have ended the story? Think of three different ways the story could have ended to suggest these three viewpoints:

   a   women should not marry men who fight over them

   b   men should not fall in love with women just because they are pretty

   c   love at first sight is not always true love.

The Tinker's Curse
by Joan Aiken

1 The writer does not tell us where this story is set – but there are some dialect words and other details that give us clues. Can you work out in which country the story takes place? Write down the clues that helped you.

2 Why do you think the writer decided that all the characters should speak in rhyme?

3 Do you think the Tinker deserved the way he was treated by the robber and his wife? Find a quotation to support your point of view, then write a sentence or two explaining how the writer has made you feel this.

4 Which other characters in the story are 'good'? Which characters are 'bad'? Choose two good characters and two bad characters; for each one, find a quotation and write an explanation, as you did for question 3.

5 Some characters change their attitudes and behaviour towards others during the story. What makes them change? What is the story suggesting about the way we should treat other people?

The Star-Child
by Oscar Wilde

1 Everything that the Star-Child does has a consequence. Make a list of his actions, good and bad – and the punishment or reward he receives. Use a table like this:

Cause	Effect
The Star-Child throws stones at the poor and laughs at the ugly.	People laugh at the Star-Child's ugliness and throw stones at him.
The Star-Child blinds moles, throws stones at lepers.	

2 What do you notice about the Star-Child's behaviour and its consequences during the course of the story?

3 What moral or lesson do you think the writer wants us to learn from this story?

4 The Star-Child's story ends happily – but the story itself does not. Why do you think the writer has done this? Does it change your answer to question 3 above?

5 Using note form, plan the story of the next king – the one we are told came after the Star-Child. What are his evil actions? What are the consequences? How does his story end?